Contents

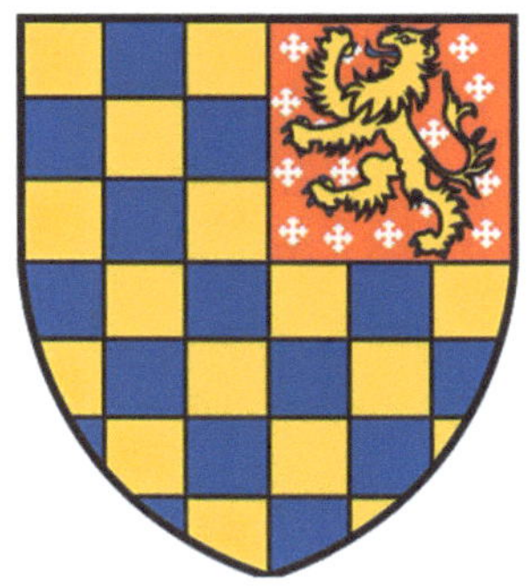

Preface

Seth Gopin

Thomas Paine is an elusive, often contradictory figure. He had little formal education, yet his prose forms the bedrock of 18th-century revolutionary thought. He was never elected to any public office, yet he changed the course of political history on two continents. He had few roots and was almost a stateless soul, yet he belonged and was accepted everywhere. He was said to be gruff and unpleasant, yet he represented best the ideals of the late eighteenth-century Enlightenment. He has few statues or monuments erected to him in the United States, yet he is an important founding father of the country. Even today, he is still misunderstood and there are lacuna in his life despite the many scholarly tomes written about him.

The year 2009 was the 200th anniversary of Paine's death, and a ten-day festival in Lewes was held to highlight a story that has never been told - the six formative years in which Paine lived and worked in this East Sussex town.

On Heritage Day, 2008, while waiting for a tour of historic Lewes House, the ever-friendly Ann Spike of the Lewes District Council was curious about the two Americans sitting in the Garden Room, awaiting the tour. Once she learned that we were not only newly arrived to England but were academics overseeing an American study abroad program and were settling into a beautiful home on St. Anne's Crescent in Lewes, she exclaimed, *"We are just setting up a festival to celebrate Tom Paine who lived right here in Lewes."* Ann continued, *"Wouldn't it be grand if we could establish some link between your university and Lewes during the celebration."*

Oddly enough, one of Paine's abodes in the colonies in 1776, a fateful year in American history if there ever was one, was in New Brunswick, the home of Rutgers University, my school. The house in which Paine had sought refuge from British troops still stands today, next to the New Brunswick Library. Rutgers holds a special place in American higher education because it was one of the colonial colleges founded in 1766 by a royal charter from George III. I had passed Paine's home for almost 20 years and never thought much of it. So, the coincidence of living in two places—Lewes and New Brunswick—where Thomas Paine also had lived was too great an opportunity to pass up. In good American fashion, I said, "*Let's talk.*"

Paul Myles, the organizer of the festival, and I were soon introduced to each other. During a four-hour walk along the Downs we talked about Thomas Paine, the festival, and shared thoughts about how to approach the material. As demonstrated by the previous exhibitions he had organized, *Rodin in Lewes, Henry Moore Land and Sea,* and *With the Grain: Wood Sculpture by David Nash*, Paul is the master of organizing. He knows how to bring together the right people to get the right results. Clearly, tackling Paine in Lewes was going to be his new challenge.

We were absolutely convinced that the key to understanding Thomas Paine were his Lewes years. The six years that Paine lived, married, evolved, and wrote in Lewes surely had to be a formative time in his life. How could Paine have travelled from Lewes to the New World and written *Common Sense* within a year of his arrival if he had not already had the proper "tools" at hand?

Dr. Colin Brent, beloved Lewes historian par excellence, was the right person to look at Paine through the prism of Lewes' fascinating and complicated history. Eminent scholars from both sides of the Atlantic have poured through Lewes' archives looking for traces of Paine and each came away with basically the same material that could be found in almost any primer on Paine. Once each word and document were put through the "filter" of Lewes as understood by Colin Brent, the story of Paine in Lewes unfolded before our eyes. It was a story that has been misunderstood and misinterpreted by previous scholars, and our weekly meetings were lively and exciting.

Through providence and careful research, Paul Myles unearthed in the British Library an obscure, self-published book about Paine by George Hindmarch. Hindmarch, a 20th-century excise officer, spent a lifetime looking at a remarkable but obscure work of Paine, *The Case of the Officers of Excise*. Hindmarch's account, from the viewpoint of an excise officer, about Paine's earliest pamphlet is both fascinating and revealing. Hindmarch's widow sent Paul a treasure trove of primary documents that led to a still deeper understanding of Paine in Lewes.

Another story never told before the 2009 Festival is that of another local man who, like Paine, helped form the United States and change the course of world events. Thomas Gage was Commander in Chief of the British Forces in the North America Colonies at the beginning of the American Revolution, his family ancestral home was at Firle, a short 5 miles from Lewes. Like Paine, Gage was a major protagonist in the drama of events that lead to the American revolution, albeit in the opposite camp. Gage and Paine's lives overlapped in England and in the colonies. Deborah Gage recounts the story of the two men. As she rightly comments, "*Thomas Gage was a victim of circumstance: in the wrong place at the wrong time.*" I would add, conversely, Paine was consistently in the right place at the right time.

Paine was not an arcane writer whose ideas and prose appealed to the elite, then and now. Au contraire, Paine's ideals and words are as much alive today as they were 200 years ago. If proof be needed, the 44th president of the United States, Barack Obama, invoked Paine in his inaugural address. Obama's speech ended with a long quotation from Paine's writing that George Washington had ordered to be read to his troops when the revolt looked bleak for the Colonists: *"Let it be told to the future world ... that in the depth of winter, when nothing but hope and virtue could survive ... that the city and the country, alarmed at one common danger, came forth to meet it "* The passage comes from Paine's critical December 1776 *The American Crisis*, which famously begins: "These are the times that try men's souls."

In the decade since the Lewes Festival, Paul Myles has unearthed primary sources related to Paine in Lewes. He has delved into Lewes' 18th-century *Sussex Weekly Advertiser or Lewes Journal*, not only to determine Paine's presence in the local paper but also to gain insight into what Paine was reading and what news he had access to. The analysis of this newspaper has added significantly to our understanding of East Sussex in the 18th century. And Myles' recent publication, *The Rise of Thomas Paine and The Case of the Officers of Excise*, is a carefully researched work which advances how we are to understand Paine's origins and considers in depth an obscure and mis-understood work that Paine wrote while living in Lewes, *The Case of the Officers of Excise*.

Thomas Paine in Lewes (1768-1774): A Prelude to American Independence, with essays by Colin Brent, Deborah Gage, and Paul Myles, is about much more than an uncommon pamphleteer or a misunderstood general; it is also the story of Lewes and how this special town helped form a new world.

Seth Gopin, New York

February 2020

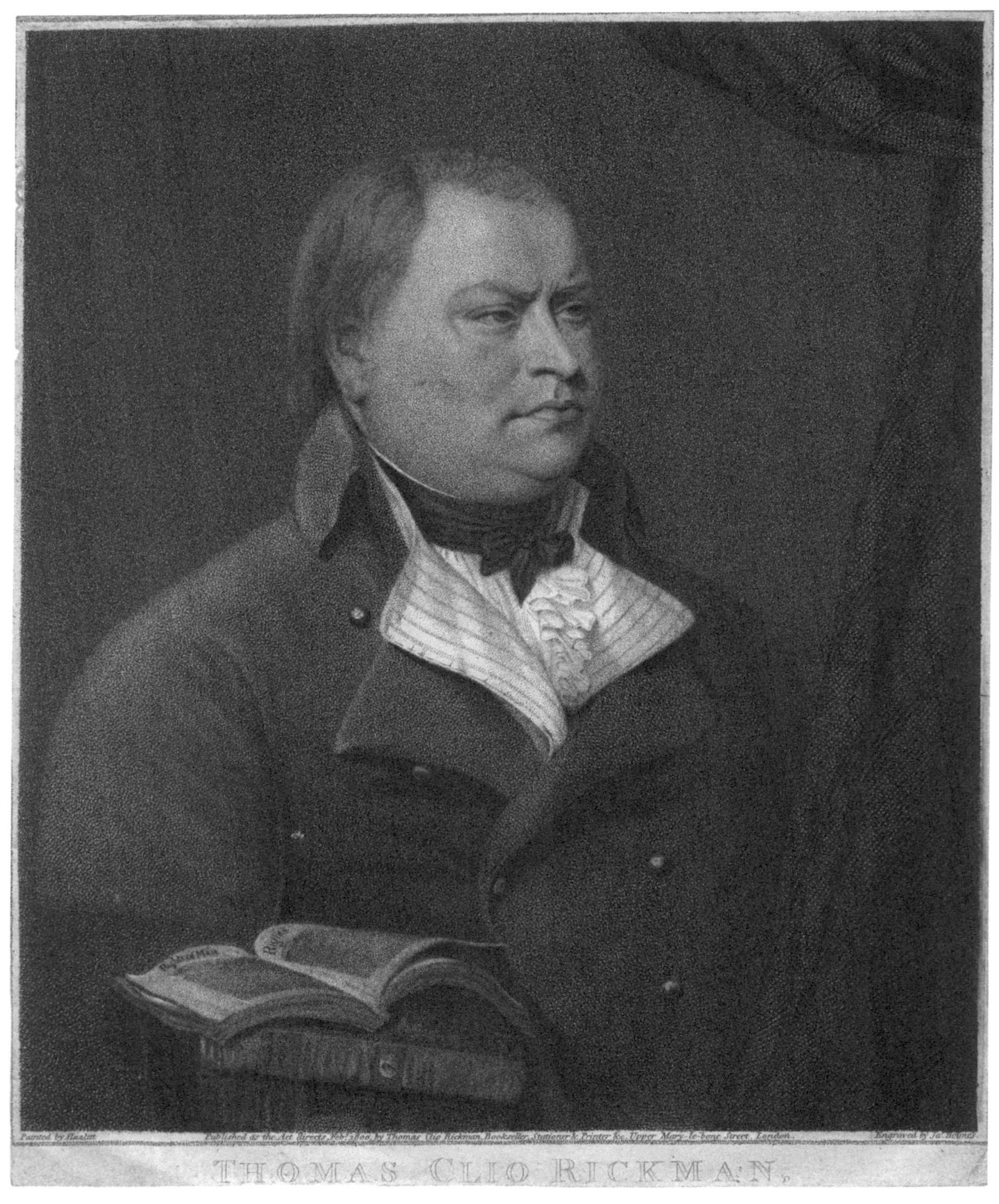

Thomas Clio Rickman © NPG

Paine's Debt To Lewes

Colin Brent

It is over two hundred years since Tom Paine died in 1809 at Greenwich, a village near New York. Many believe he was the greatest English political pamphleteer who ever lived. And it was soon after he left Lewes for America in May 1774 that he wrote his *Common Sense*, which convinced our American colonists they should fight for Independence, for a federal Republic guaranteeing civil liberties and freedom of religion. *The sun never shined on a cause of greater worth...Now is the seed time of continental union, faith and honour.* Soon after, his *Crisis* bulletins steadied nerves when Washington retreated to Valley Forge. *These are the times that try men's souls. The summer soldier and the sunshine patriot will, in this crisis, shrink from the service of their country; but he that stands it now, deserves the love and thanks of man and woman.* Stirring stuff! No wonder President-elect Obama highjacked a sentence or two for his inauguration speech.

After American Independence was won in 1783, Paine returned to England with his pioneer design for a cast-iron river bridge. But then the fall of the Bastille and Revolution in France inspired his *Rights of Man*. British working-class Radicals bought thousands of cheap copies in 1791-3 — and no wonder! His pamphlet rubbished hereditary monarchies and aristocracies as irrational, expensive and militarist. It predicted instead an alliance of new Republics, in America, France and Britain, bringing an era of Atlantic harmony, trade and prosperity, and a Peace Dividend to be spent on a Welfare State. The cost of the child benefits, sick pay and old-age pensions were precisely calculated. William Pitt and his royalist ministers were understandably furious and Paine fled to France, being promptly elected to its National Convention.

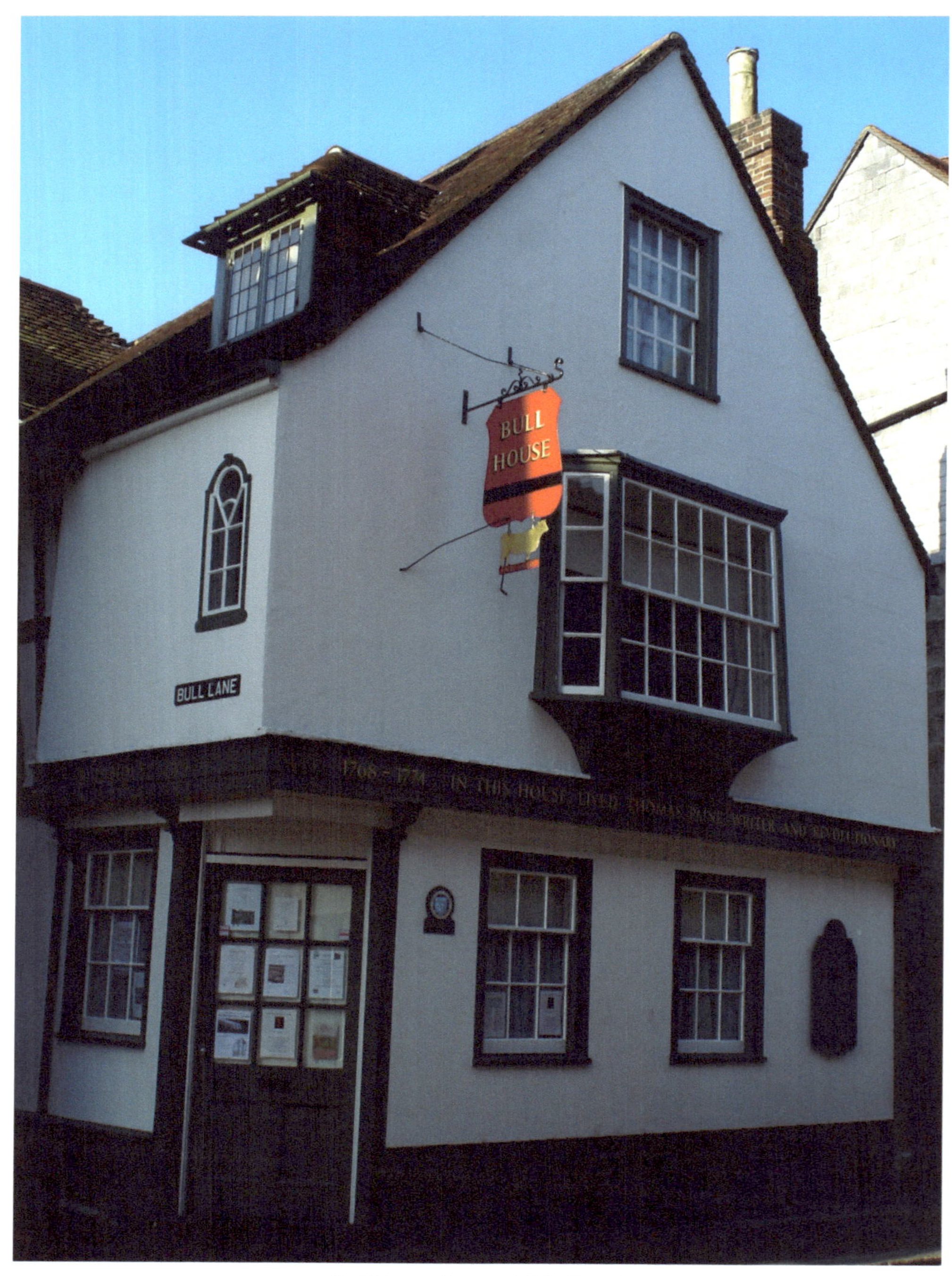

Bull House Lewes High Street

Paine's Debt to Lewes by Colin Brent

But then he was imprisoned, and nearly guillotined, for voting against the execution of Louis XVI. Meanwhile in his *Age of Reason* he argued that God existed, but that proofs put forward by Christians, Jews and Moslems did not hold water. So, after his return to New York in 1802, American Evangelists reviled him as an atheist – a slur that stuck for a century.

Paine left Lewes in 1774 to begin writing these pamphlets that changed American and British history when he was already thirty-seven. He sailed to Philadelphia with a rich store of experience. England moulded him. And for six solid years, from March 1768, he lived in Lewes, most of the time at Bull House, nearly opposite St Michael's church in the High Street. But, before we explore these years, what of Paine's life before Lewes? He was born in 1737 at Thetford, a borough town in Norfolk. His father, a Quaker, was a self-employed corset-maker. His mother was C. of E., the daughter of the town clerk. So, there were two faiths in one household. After a commercial course at the grammar school followed a seven-year apprenticeship with his father – like Shakespeare and Dickens, Paine had little Latin and less Greek. Breaking free from Thetford, he served for six months in 1757 on a licensed privateer, the *King of Prussia*. But then for ten years he drifted. He tried corset-making at Dover and at Sandwich. He married, but his wife died. He went back to Thetford. Joining the Excise, he worked at Grantham and was sacked at Alford. He returned to corset-making, at Diss. Re-admitted to the Excise, he turned down a post at Grampound in Cornwall, and bided his time teaching English at private schools in London, before arriving at Bull House in March 1768 as a 'riding' excise officer in the Lewes Division. Its official base was the *White Hart*.

His patience was rewarded, for Lewes certainly suited him. After years of drift, false starts and failure, he settled down and explored life as an excise officer, grocer and tobacconist, householder, ratepayer, burgess, debater and bowler. Above all, Lewes was vibrantly prosperous. Its corn and livestock markets flourished. Onto the wharves at Cliffe groceries, wine and consumer goods were unloaded from London, timber from the Baltic, coal from Newcastle. Moreover, being the county town of eastern Sussex it hosted the royal judges at the summer assizes and the magistrates at quarter sessions. It nurtured a newspaper, the *Sussex Weekly Advertiser or Lewes Journal.* So the High Street was lined with vintners, grocers and butchers, saddlers, gunsmiths and watchmakers, drapers, milliners and shoemakers. *The Bear,* the *Star,* the *White Hart* and the *White Horse* excelled as hostelries. Professional men – physicians and surgeons, lawyers, clergy and academy-owners - abounded. Dash and excitement were supplied by the summer races, the touring theatre companies and the balls at the Assembly Room when the moon was full. Cash and expertise were also exported to fuel the booming local sea-resort of Brightelmstone.

And Lewes was very alive politically. As a borough it returned two members to parliament. But it had no royal charter. No mayor, corporation and freemen ruled the roost and monopolised local trade. Instead, all male householders who paid their parish poor rate could vote, meaning there were several hundred electors, many of them affluent. And in March 1768, the very month Paine arrived, they elected two enlightened landowners as their MPs. Thomas Hay of Glyndeborne and Thomas Hampden of Glynde were neighbours. Both voted in the Commons against attempts by the king's ministers to imprison, silence or expel their fellow MP, John Wilkes, the great champion of civil liberties. And Paine maybe joined the welcome given him in August 1770. As the *Lewes Journal* reported, after Wilkes arrived at the *Star,* with his daughter: *the bells in our several churches were immediately rung, and vast crowds of people assembled to see the great patriot, at whom they expressed their pleasure by joyful acclamations. Every mark of real esteem was shown him by the inhabitants that could be expressed to a gentleman so highly deserving*

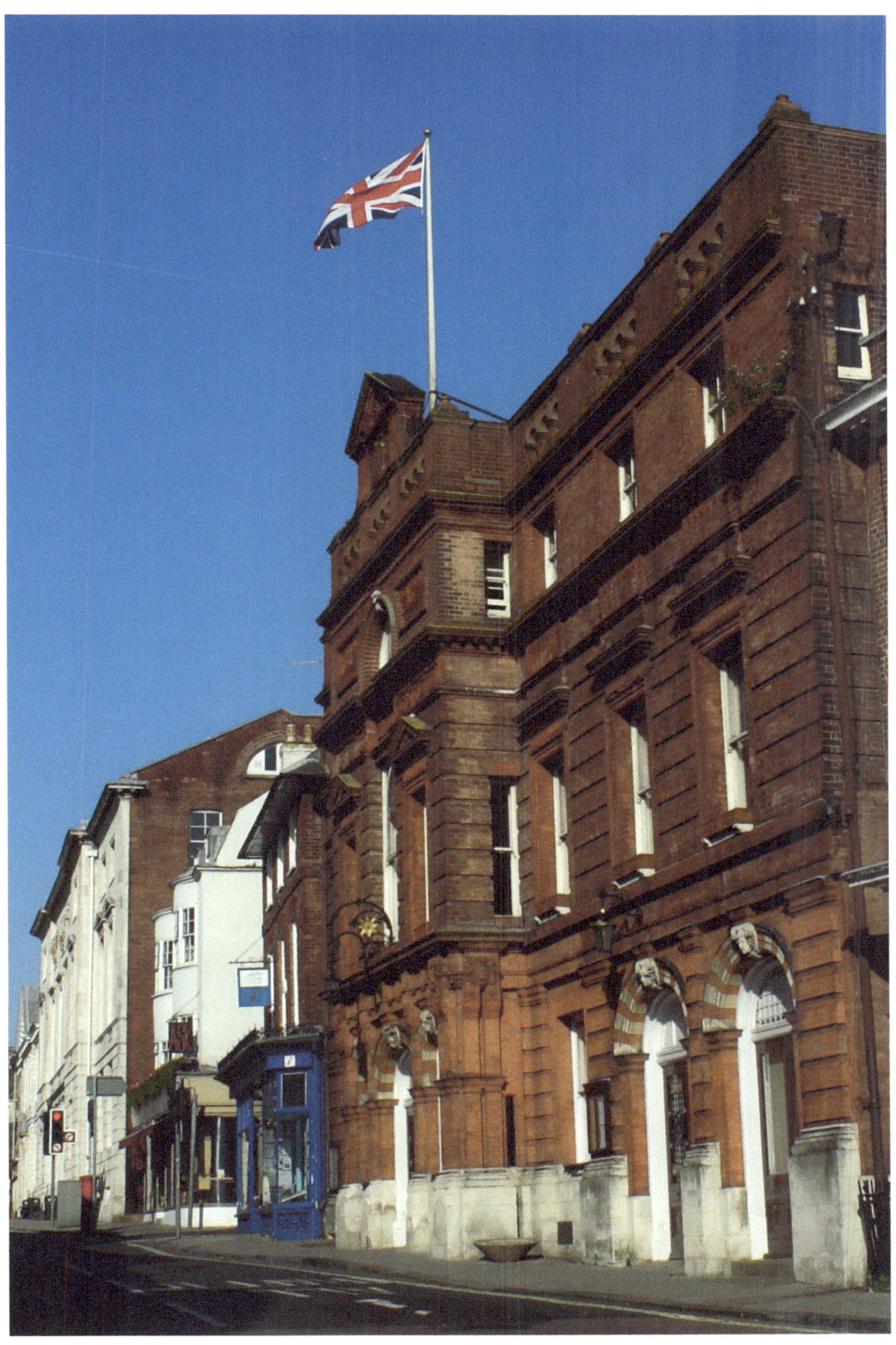

Lewes Town Hall - formerly the Star Inn

the public Regard. As for the power of popular opinion, the *Journal* also reported in 1773, and Paine perhaps witnessed that local magistrates were 'roughly used' when they tried to stop Bonfire Boys building their traditional immense pile of faggots on School Hill.

So Lewes life undoubtedly suited Paine and, though a seasoned drifter, he soon adapted to it. Luckily his landlord quickly befriended him. Samuel Ollive was a man of parts. A grocer and tobacconist, he owned Bull House and a farm at Barcombe. He was the current Senior High Constable. He was a pillar of the wealthy Dissenting chapel at Westgate. His father John had been the pastor there. He subscribed to a 'liberal' Christian magazine edited by Doctor Doddridge. Samuel also intended that after his death, which occurred in July 1769, his daughter and three sons should 'share and share alike' his legacy, subject to his widow's life interest - like Paine he rejected primogeniture. But his sons, watchmakers by trade, did not want the business. So in September the former lodger and Elizabeth, the late landlord's daughter, intrepidly advertised in the *Journal* that, jointly, they would continue to sell at Bull House *all sorts of Tobacco, Snuff, Cheese, Butter and Home-made Bacon, with every Article of Grocery (Tea excepted) Wholesale and Retail, at the lowest Prices.* Logically, too, in March 1771 they married in St. Michael's church, witnessed by Henry Verral who managed the coffee house and assembly room. So it was as his mother-in-law's tenant, responsible only for repairs, that he informed the trustees of Westgate chapel, which structurally adjoined Bull House: *I cannot think myself empowered to give any answers concerning the filling up of the [shared] door which you complain of.* But he did agree to pay them a shilling a year for allowing into their yard *the droppings of Rain which fall from a New Building lately erected by me.*

As a resident, householder and ratepayer in Lewes, Paine had six years in which to experience a vital truth, which he reiterated thereafter to Americans and Britons alike: *In England the whole of the*

          Paine's Debt to Lewes by Colin Brent

civil government is executed by the people of every town and county, by means of parish officers, magistrates, quarter sessions, juries and assize: in effect republican government. He could observe, of course, at the Town Hall in the High Street the business at the summer assizes and the quarter sessions, attracting a stream of parish constables, jurors and witnesses. As a ratepayer in St Michael's parish he attended vestry meetings to monitor spending by its elected 'parish officers' - the churchwardens and the overseers who relieved the poor and managed the almshouse. And Paine himself served as a jury man, very assiduously indeed, at all five of the annual October meetings of the Lewes court leet held between 1769 and 1773. Other enthusiasts were his friend Henry Verrall, the coffee house keeper, and Thomas Scrase, the landlord of the *White Hart.* The jury, usually about twenty strong, checked the accounts of the two High Constables and then elected two new ones. These officers kept law and order in the borough, locked suspects up in the West Gate, and acted as Returning Officers at parliamentary elections. Paine and about a hundred other householders also attended an annual town meeting to authorise a borough rate. As well, in 1772, they urged the High Constables to keep wheel barrows and sledges off the pavements.

Besides experiencing England's *republican government* for six years in Lewes, Paine also honed his debating skills. Clio Rickman's admiring biography, compiled in Paine's defence about thirty years later, states that *He lived in habits of intimacy with a very respectable, sensible and convivial set of acquaintance, who were entertained with his witty sallies, and informed by his more serious conversations. ... He was tenacious of his opinions, which were bold, acute, and independent, and which he maintained with ardour, elegance and argument.* Much of this debate, Rickman claimed, occurred at *the White Hart evening club.* This was *a social and intelligent circle who, out of fun, seeing that disputes often ran very warm and high, frequently had what they called the 'Headstrong Book'. [Last heard of in 1811]. This was no other than an old Greek*

Homer which was sent the morning after a debate vehemently maintained, to the most obstinate haranguer of the Club; this book had the following title, as implying that Mr. Paine the best deserved and the most frequently obtained it. The HEADSTRONG BOOK or ORIGINAL BOOK OF OBSTINACY ... revised and corrected by Thomas Paine.

Clio Rickman, of course, gathered this second hand. He was born in 1761 at Cliffe, near today's *John Harvey* tavern, his father being a Quaker corn dealer. But he was away training to be a surgeon till he returned home in 1779, unqualified, but keen on versifying and Voltaire. He fell out with the Quakers, traded tin plate in Barcelona and set up in London as a Radical bookseller. He met Paine on his return from America. Indeed his hero lodged over the bookshop while penning part two of *Rights of Man* in 1792. His host later fixed to the table a brass plate celebrating that seminal event. Their friendship endured. In 1802 at Le Havre Clio waved Paine goodbye when he sailed back to America and in 1809 Paine left him part of his property.

Paine also found time to relax at Lewes. As William Lee, the faintly preposterous editor of the *Lewes Journal*, condescendingly reminisced in 1794: *He was very fond of amusing himself, and others, in skating parties on the ice, where, from his intrepid spirit in exploring the slippery surface, he was distinguished by the title of Commodore. Tom was likewise the hero of our Bowling-green, where he observed much more exactness with the measuring-stick, than he was accustomed to be at the beer-barrel with his dipping-rule.* And a rare reminiscence by Paine recalled a discussion at Lewes, over punch, after of a game of bowls. A *Mr Verril*, quite possibly Henry Verrall, the coffee house keeper, remarked that the *king of Prussia was the best fellow in the world for a king, he had so much of the devil in him. Apparently, from this Paine deduced that if it were necessary for a king to have so much of the devil in him, kings might very beneficially be dispensed with.*

          Paine's Debt to Lewes by Colin Brent

So Paine was surely wise to reject a post at Grampound, a decaying Cornish backwater. The vibrant 'republican' culture of Lewes must have suited much better the embryonic political pamphleteer. Indeed, according to Rickman, Paine penned there *several excellent little pieces in prose and verse*, two of them published in his *Pennsylvania Magazine* in 1775. Both satirised the status quo. *Farmer Short's Dog Porter* spun an absurd fable about three fatuous magistrates condemning a dog to hang for chasing a hare into a pond where it drowned; it also exposed the arbitrariness of the anti-poaching laws. *The Death of General Wolfe*, set to music and immensely popular, mocked the bombastic, worn-out Heroic style, larded with Classical allusion, used to acclaim Great Men.

And maybe two letters to the *Lewes Journal*, signed HUMANUS, were also written by Paine, who went on to design his own iron bridge, and to denounce in *Rights of Man* the evil settlement laws when setting out his plan for a Welfare State: *The dying poor will not be dragged from place to place to breathe their last, as a reprisal of parish upon parish.* The first letter described in detail a fire escape, *a machine lately invented for the preservation of lives by fire*, and ended with a plea, *let Reason go on in its proper course.* The second letter denounced the fate of a near neighbour of Paine's, a metalworker, William Weston, aged thirty five: a *poor dying man brought* [to St Michael's parish] *on Wednesday evening last, in a small, open cart, having nothing to shelter him from the inclement weather, but a little straw, lightly strewed over him, and in which shameful manner, it appeared, he had been passed on the Vagrant Act, from a parish in Yorkshire, where he was taken ill.... every person present at the removal of the straw was struck with horror and amazement, when the shocking spectacle was displayed to their view, emaciated, and unable to move himself, with little other covering than what Nature had given him, except (if I may be allowed the expression) a coat of Vermin, which was eagerly devouring him alive. ...In such a state of torment had this poor miserable creature lain for thirty-six days.* Despite the efforts of his Lewes friends, the letter concludes, he was buried the following Friday.

And it was at Lewes, of course, that Paine wrote his first pamphlet, *The Case of the Officers of Excise*. He set out in concise detail why their salaries were too low. He coolly conceded that as a result negligence and corruption were rife. A pay rise would restore efficiency and stem a steady loss of government revenue. Flashes of imagination temper the remorseless logic. *True Honesty is sentimental, and the Practice of it dependent on Circumstance, on avoiding the cold Regions of Want, the Circle of Polar Poverty. The officers are shut out from the general Blessing – They behold it like a Map of Peru.* The facts, the logic and the fire – *The Case* heralds *Common Sense*.

Paine's departure from Lewes, from his wife and from the Excise, in the spring of 1774 were observed by William Carver, a young blacksmith baptised at Southover in 1755. *He went to school with Miss Ollive* [Paine's wife], perhaps as her pupil; she had been a *teacher to Mrs. Ridge.* In 1790 when he voted for two 'liberal' candidates at the borough election, he lived at the top of St Martin's Lane on the west side. In 1794 he migrated to New York where he became *a most strenuous advocate … of Mr Paine's political and religious principles.* Indeed for several months in 1806, like Samuel Ollive and Clio Rickman before him, he became his highly supportive landlord. Paine, after being jailed in France and then abused by American Evangelicals, had declined in health and taken somewhat to the bottle. So this final service from a Lewesian was a timely one.

Bibliography

Colin Brent, *Thirty something: Thomas Paine at Bull House in Lewes 1768-74- Six Formative Years,* Sussex Archaeological Collection, Vol. 147 (2009)

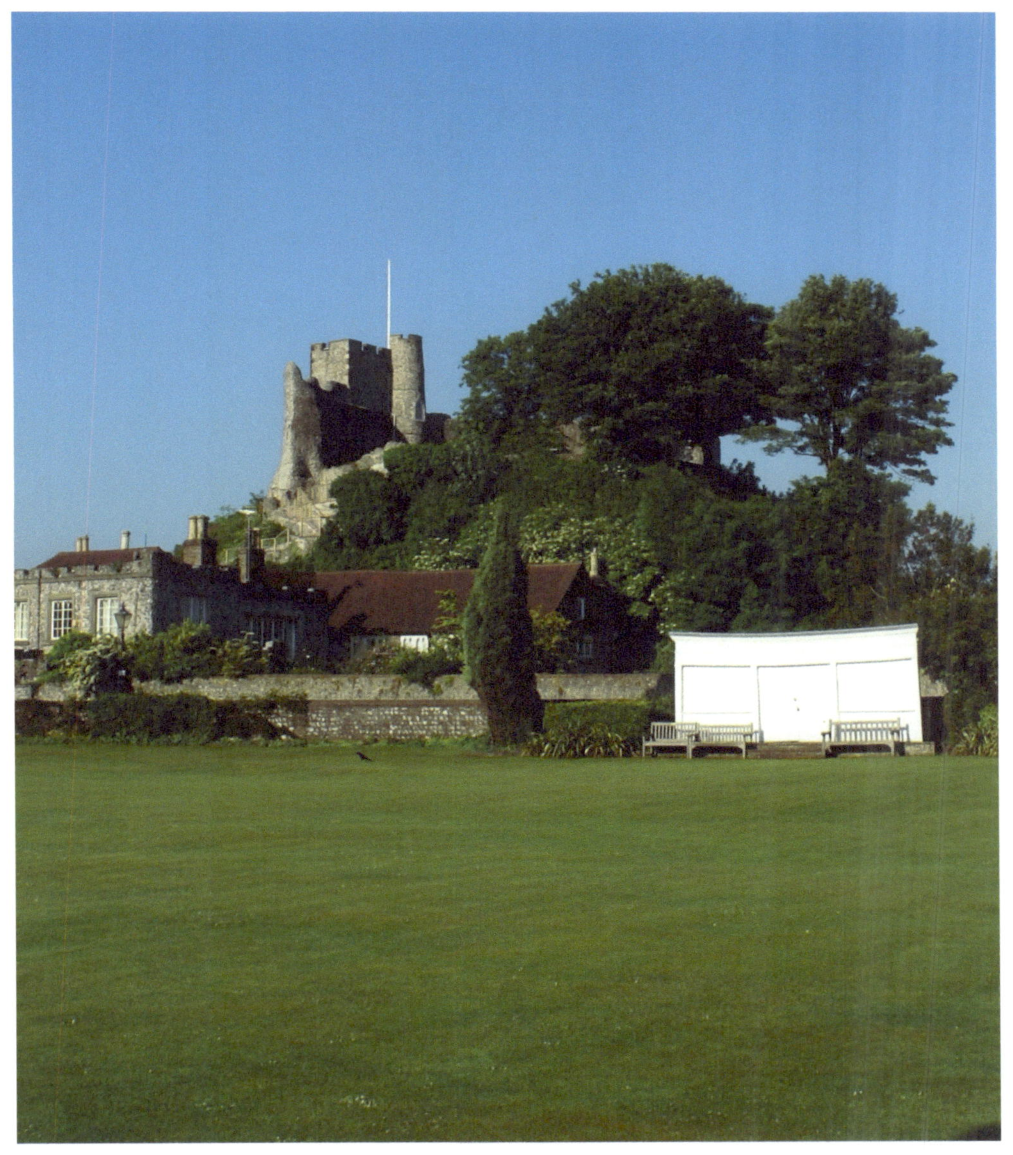

Lewes Bowling Green

THE CASE

OF THE

OFFICERS

OF

EXCISE;

With REMARKS on the

QUALIFICATIONS

OF

OFFICERS;

AND ON THE

Numerous EVILS arising to the

REVENUE,

From the INSUFFICIENCY of the

PRESENT SALARY.

Humbly addressed to the

Hon. and Right Hon. the MEMBERS

OF

Both HOUSES of PARLIAMENT.

Thomas Paine's Lewes Pamphlet

Paul Myles

*T*here was vagueness about the time that Thomas Paine spent in Lewes. Many said he was not born here, so why make a fuss? It was against this backdrop that a small research team started in early 2008. Dr Colin Brent agreed to help; I was fresh out of university as a mature student and a stroke of good fortune introduced Dr Seth Gopin, an American art historian and director of abroad studies for Rutgers University of New Jersey. It was an interesting mix, Colin, the eminent local historian, Seth from America, and myself from the discipline of psychology at the University of Sussex. Seth's question was, how did Paine know so much when he wrote the pamphlet *Common Sense* that incited the colonists to the War of Independence just 17 months after leaving Lewes? My view was that a developmental process seemed to be missing.

Oldys wrote the first biography of Paine in 1791 at the behest of the Pitt government. The book was well researched, but George Chalmers, the real name of the author, never missed an opportunity to defame Paine. And so the mud stuck, and has remained stuck in many minds for the last two hundred years.

Thomas Paine wrote *The Case of the Officers of Excise*, and William Lee, proprietor of the Lewes Journal, printed four thousand copies in Lewes. But there was no original to hand, not one left in Lewes. Eventually a scan of the 1772 original was found. Two later published versions, one in 1792 by J. S. Jordan with an anonymous forward, and one in 1817 by W. T. Sherwin were found. This was becoming interesting, after Paine's fame was established in America, at least two individuals had picked up on the importance of the Lewes document. In the forward of Jordan's publication the writer noted that *The Case of the Officers of Excise* was Paine's *first literary attempt* and that his *virgin effort discovers a great share of that vigour and subtlety of mind.*

Here is the final resounding paragraph of Thomas Paine's first pamphlet, clearly looking forward to a time when corruption of the Officers of Excise would be eliminated by fair pay and conditions:

An augmentation of salary sufficient to enable them to live honestly, and competently would produce more good effect than all the laws of the land can enforce. The generality of such frauds as the officers have been detected in have appeared of a nature as remote from inherent dishonesty as a temporary illness is from an incurable disease. Surrounded with want, children and despair, what can the husband or the father do? No laws compel like nature - no connections bind like blood.
With an addition of salary the excise would wear a new aspect, and recover its former constitution. Languor and neglect would give place to care and cheerfulness. Men of reputation and abilities would seek after it, and finding a comfortable maintenance, would stick to it. The unworthy and the incapable would be rejected; the power of superiors be re-established, and laws and instructions receive new force. The officers would be secured from the temptations of poverty, and the revenue from the evils of it; the cure would be as extensive as the complaint, and new health out-root the present corruptions.

Whilst searching for *The Case of The Officers of Excise* another publication with the title *The Case of the King of England and his Officers of Excise* published privately by George Hindmarch in 1998, showed on the British library listing. The remaining copies were found with the help of Robert Morell, the acting secretary of the national Thomas Paine Society. The claims within this book are nothing short of extraordinary. George Hindmarch died in 2006; his research material was generously made available by the Thomas

Paine Society on the proviso that it was passed to East Sussex Record Office. George was an exciseman and had interpreted the excise archive entries about Paine and his superior officers with an exciseman's eye.

Hindmarch's interpretation told a story in contradiction to previous accounts. He showed us that Paine was discharged initially in Alford not for corruption, but for whistleblowing, describing an eighteenth century world that had only known corruption in the excise service. The writings of Graham Smith, H M Customs and Excise librarian and archivist, support this, *Defoe noted that smuggling and rogueing is the reigning commerce from the mouth of the Thames to Cornwall, very few collectors were prepared to make a stand against this (1724).*

Smith noted that the expense of printing and distributing 4000 copies of the Case of the Officers of Excise would have required formal, central organisation. Hindmarch argued that this must have been from London. Hindmarch and Smith had both, as excisemen, spotted what other biographers had missed to date. The main clue has always been there in a letter Paine wrote to Oliver Goldsmith, the famous poet and playwright, stating about his own first pamphlet, *It is my first and only attempt, and even now I should not have undertaken it, had I not been particularly applied to by some of my superiors in office.*

The Lewes pamphlet was eclipsed by the huge events of the American and French revolutions, even in Paine's mind, for he never referred to it again. But revolution does not always require bloodletting, the changes effected by *The Case of The Officers of Excise* have been deeper than hitherto realised. Graham Smith acknowledged Paine's contribution to the well being of officers through the Lewes pamphlet. The office of excise eventually accepted all of the proposals made by Paine. It took time though; the distressing enforced periodic transference of officers was finally abolished in 1857, eighty-five years after the pamphlet was distributed. It is ironic that Thomas Paine made such positive contributions to the service that his eventual detractors were most dependent on.

Hindmarch took us back to 1698, William of Orange nearly went back to Holland as he was not being paid enough to be a King of England, Ireland and Scotland. The civil list was created at this point in time to resolve this delicate issue, the Crown being granted certain revenues mainly from excise and customs. This was not a rolling deal but negotiated at the start of each reign. The tensions locked within the new tripartite system, the Crown, Lords and Commons persist to this day, but it was particularly difficult for the naïve young George III, whose settlement was low with no adjustment for inflation. The King immediately started to run up debts.

The civil list was used to defray the expenses of the civil service, which included personal and household expenses. Pensions were also paid from the civil list, a pension effectively gagging Dr Samuel Johnson who said *But, Sir, I think that the pleasure of cursing the House of Hanover, and drinking King James's health, are amply overbalanced by three hundred pounds a year.*

Some startling facts emerged, by the time Paine came to Lewes, the excise wages paid from the civil list had been frozen for nearly a hundred years. King George III had short-changed himself in his initial settlement with Parliament. Both the King and the officers of excise were short of cash in a period of high inflation. The King had to go to Parliament to liquidate his debts and the revenue officers were corrupt in order to survive. The King of England and his officers of excise were trapped in a spiralling problem. After his arrival in Lewes, Paine was selected to join a committee of eight officers of excise to jointly petition the commissioners of Excise for better pay and conditions. The members were:

Thomas Sykes	of	London	(Calicoes)
William May	of	Salisbury	
Henry Holland	of	Nottingham	
Thomas Gray	of	London	(Distilleries)
John Grosse	of	Newcastle	
Richard Ayling	of	London	(Breweries)
Thomas Pattinson	of	Gravesend and Rochester	
Thomas Pain	of	Lewes	

It now started to appear that there was some identifiable process to Thomas Paine's development from a humble outrider to world commentator. Smith indicated that this committee was assembled from above, Hindmarch went further and claimed that George Lewis Scott, one of the commissioners on the board of Excise, previously tutor to the young King George III, acted with the King's knowledge in this matter. Smith noted that Scott was a great mathematician and introduced new ideas to the revenue, tantalisingly he did not cite Paine's pamphlet.

Thomas Paine penned 'ic *The Case of the Officers of Excise*' and wrote with one voice for two thousand seven hundred officers. Every officer of excise signed a petition for the first mass campaign of this kind. Paine wrote to Goldsmith from the Excise Coffee House in Broad Street, *A petition for this purpose has been translated through every part of the kingdom, and signed by all the officers therein. A subscription of three shillings per officer is raised, amounting to upwards of £500, for supporting the expenses,* on December the 21st, 1772. Paine was obviously given leave from Lewes to gather intelligence in the London excise office.

 The implications of the foregoing are weighty, *The Case of the Officers of Excise* is the first civil service unionisation, and foreshadowed the green and white paper lobbying system of the British parliament. It proposed an impeccable civil service; four thousand copies were distributed, one to every officer of excise, every member of both houses of parliament and important businessmen of the day. It was forwarded to the treasury by the nine members of the excise board. What we can see in this pamphlet is his urgent, cogent, witty and elegant prose, which he used with such devastating effect in *Common Sense,* the pamphlet that incited the War of Independence just seventeen months after he left Lewes.

But Paine was not revolutionary as an advocate for better pay and conditions. His whole argument was for improvements to the status quo. He never argued for getting rid of the Crown, he argued in the King's favour. Improve pay and conditions and the whole country will thrive. He was in support of his fellow officers of excise and the country in its entirety. Paine cut his literary teeth in Lewes, and he did it in the service of his King.

Several questions continue to nag. Paine was discharged twice from the revenue, in Alford and Lewes. How was Paine reinstated into the excise office so expeditiously? How could Paine reject the first post offered at Grampound after his restoration to the revenue? Why and how was Paine singled out to be on a committee of eight prior to the petition and the pamphlet? Why was he discharged from his post from Lewes if he was in the service of his superiors in the writing of *The Case of the Officers of Excise?*

Hindmarch pointed out that Swallow, Paine's superior officer in Alford, after an anonymous complaint, was demoted after he was found using Paine's orderly books. Even Oldys, Paine's malicious but exacting first biographer notes: *Whether while he rode as an exciseman at Alford his practices had been misrepresented by malice, tradition has not told us.* From the detailed examination of the excise record surrounding the Alford period, it appeared that Paine was discharged for not joining in the corrupt practices of the local officers of excise. Paine had stood out.

In Paine's application letter to the board of excise for reinstatement there is a revealing detail. He wrote the letter in the central excise office in London on July 3rd 1766. Paine's letter stated: *The time I enjoyed my former commission was short and unfortunate- an officer only a single year. No complaint of the least dishonesty or intemperance ever appeared against me.* He was reinstated the next day on the 4th of July 1766. The denial of any wrongdoing is clear, and must have been accepted by the board of commissioners. This was an unusually quick reinstatement, one day. This strongly implied that Earle, the officer in charge of appeals, helped Paine write the letter in the correct tone and style, vouching for him after personal interview. Earl would have been fully aware of Paine's unfair treatment at Alford.

As to Paine' eventual discharge from the service in Lewes, a substituting officer, Edward Clifford, was temporarily sent to Lewes. Clifford lodged a complaint that Paine was absent without leave. The message was rushed to London in an unseemly manner on the 6th of April 1774 in Lewes. The board's decision in London to discharge Paine was made on the 8th of April 1774. This clearly circumvented due process. The local collector, the highest excise official in Lewes, would normally have dealt with such an issue in the first instance.

There is no evidence that Paine sold up and left Lewes for any other reasons than of his own choosing. The decision to sell his assets was made before his discharge. He had settled amicably with his wife Elizabeth and discharged any current business debts with the sale of his business assets. Paine was more than likely expecting promotion due to his contact at high level with the excise service. He had been selected to be on a committee of honest excise officers, and from those had been selected to write for the whole of the excise, including his superiors, with one voice. He had been given access to information at the head office in London. He had been selected, financed and encouraged from the highest level.

Oldys commented that *George Lewis Scott could not, for the third time, obtain our author's (Paine) restoration as an officer of excise, he recommended him strongly to that great man Dr. Benjamin Franklin, as a person who could, at that epoch, be useful in America.* Oldys inadvertently gave us the strongest clue that Scott was instrumental in Paine's entire excise career. Paine was eventually thrust into high politics with the assistance of Scott, an influential member of the Board of Excise.

Paine also received praise from the clerk to the board while he was in Lewes. Clio Rickman, a former resident of Lewes and close friend, and biographer of Paine, noted that *Mr Jenner, principal clerk in the excise office, London, had several times occasion to write letters from the board of excise thanking Mr. Paine for his assiduity in his profession, and for his information and calculations forwarded to the office.*

Here lies the enigma; summary dismissal coincided with support and help from the very board that issued the notice of discharge. There were very powerful forces at play, powerful enough to bypass the local due process of investigation, powerful enough to override one of the commissioners sitting on the board. This may have represented an agreed deal to move Paine sideways to America due to political pressure from the treasury, or perhaps Paine was viewed as an expendable experiment. Paine himself acknowledged the failure of the pamphlet, noting that excisemen were not popular. What would be more attractive, a future in a new land of opportunity with a golden letter of approval from Benjamin Franklin, or a future in a provincial town, a small shop and an unconsummated marriage?

The pamphlet was ahead of its time. Paine was ahead of his time. Paine departed to America with the confidence of Scott, Franklin and a potently developed set of skills under his belt. Not dejected, but hopeful. England's loss was America's gain. Paine was to coin the phrase

The United States of America and gave the colonists the confidence to live without a King. Who knows how it would have turned out if Parliament had the wit to accept Paine's recommendations? Perhaps a small pay rise and marginally better conditions would have avoided the loss of the Americas. We shall never know. But Paine did try his best, and over a sustained period of time, for his native country. We can now see where his smouldering fury was seeded. Being let down twice by the very establishment he was enlisted by to help must have given Thomas Paine much food for thought. And the subsequences of that thought had serious world implications. Paine was unusually gifted to observe and write. Lewes society and politics were unusually accessible. These two interacting factors have had a profound effect on the political and cultural development of the Atlantic seaboard for the last two hundred years.

Bibliography:

George Hindmarch. The Case of The King of England and his Officers of Excise 1998 ISBN 0953198I
Graham Smith. *Something to declare: 1000 years of Customs and Excise* 1980 Harrap London ISBN 0245534725
George Hindmarch's research material for a biography of Paine: East Sussex Record Office Accession No. 10140

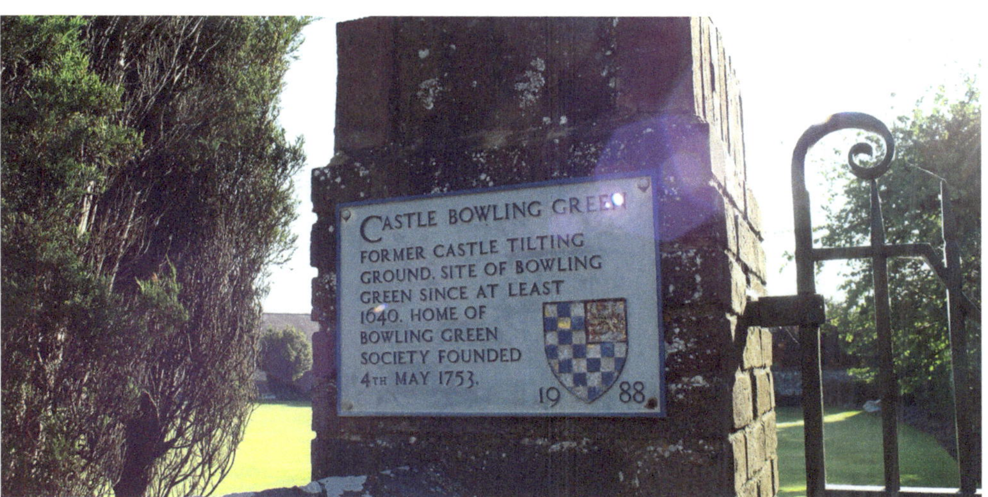

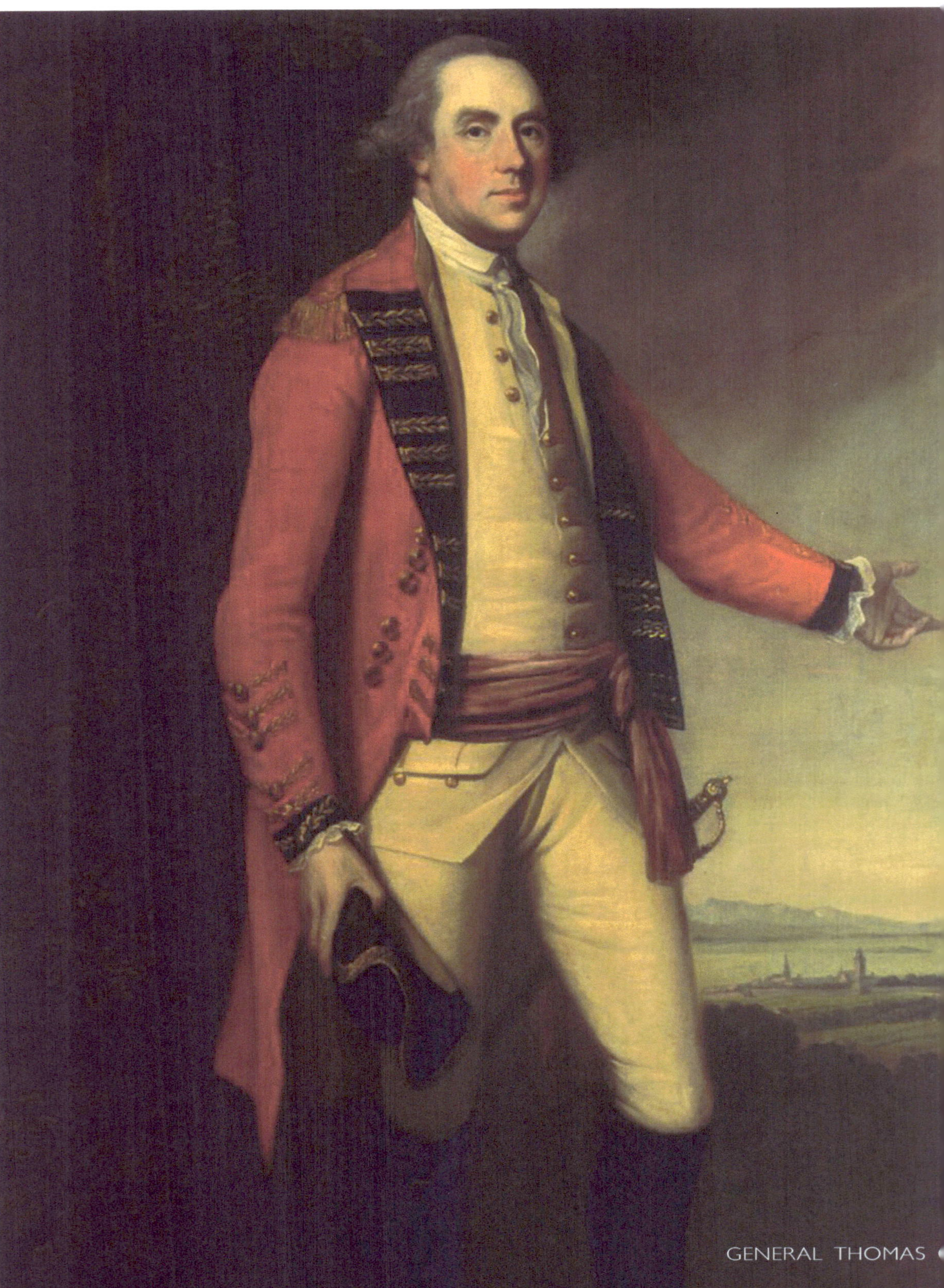

by David Martin 1775: Courtesy Firle Place Preservatio

General Gage (1721-1787) On The Eve of Revolution: A Conflict of Emotions

Deborah Gage

Thomas Gage arrived in New York in 1763 on November 16th. The next morning he took over as Commander in Chief. He would hold the post for the next twelve fateful years. William Shirley, by capturing Louisburg, began the conquest of Canada: it was finished by Wolfe and Amherst, with Thomas Gage serving under the latter. Shirley was Governor of Massachusetts from 1741 to 1749, and again from 1753 to 1756; it was Gage's duty, in a similar office, to try to carry out the insensate policy of George III, from May 1774, to October 1775, when he left Boston, jeered at and execrated, the last Governor of the Imperial connection. Thus these two men whose family homes in Sussex, England were but twelve miles apart, were prominently connected with some of the most stirring events in the histories of the United States and Canada. Was it also more than a coincidence that Paine learnt his writing skills and developed his political philosophy in Lewes just a few miles from the Gage ancestral home at Firle Place?

Thomas the first Viscount and his wife Benedicta Hall were the parents of General Thomas Gage, their second son born in 1721. Benedicta was heiress of Highmeadow, in Gloucestershire, where they lived until Thomas inherited Firle Place from his cousin, Sir William Gage, upon his death in 1744. Around the age of nine, Gage was sent to Westminster School in London, and studied there for eight years. The school had a positive effect on Thomas, and he grew up to be disciplined, hardworking, ambitious, prudent, serious, upright and well meaning. As a second son he would not inherit, leaving two choices of occupation open to him: the church or the army.

Thomas elected to pursue an army career and a King's commission was purchased for him on January 30, 1741 as a lieutenant in Colonel Cholmondeley's Regiment of Foot, where he commenced service in Ireland. Thomas Gage found army life pleasing. He enjoyed its pageantry, and took comfort in its discipline becoming a seasoned soldier, witnessing some of the most gruesome battles of the time. He was present at the British defeat at Fontenoy on May 11, 1745, one of the bloodiest conflicts of the eighteenth century, ending with 30,000 fallen men on a Flanders field, amidst scenes of horror and brutality beyond description.

A year later, in Scotland, Thomas was present for another epic slaughter. On this occasion his was the winning side at the battle of Culloden on April 27, 1746 where the Highland clans were defeated and Drumossie Moor was left carpeted with corpses. After Culloden, Gage returned to Flanders. Here he engaged in a period of peacetime soldiering, on the staff of the Earl of Albemarle, father of an old school friend.

In 1755, he was posted to America with General Edward Braddock. Gage commanded the vanguard on Braddock's expedition against the French in the Ohio Valley. On July 9, 1755, the force blindly marched into a forest ambush at Fort Duquesne, was nearly annihilated, and Braddock was killed. True to form, Gage conducted himself with courage in combat. Wounded himself, he improvised a rear guard that allowed the escape of George Washington. Gage stood out for honourable behaviour, zeal and integrity during the course of the French and Indian War that followed. It was through this time that a friendship developed between Gage and the young Virginian and fellow-officer, George Washington. They came to hold one another in respect for bravery in the face of adversity – thus was the ironic twist of fate years later, these two men would find themselves leading opposing sides.

Gage married Margaret Kemble on December 8, 1758 on the veranda of Mt. Kemble, in Morristown, she was one quarter English, one quarter Greek, one quarter Dutch and one quarter French, and was known throughout the colonies for her unusual beauty. Sensitive and exquisite, she had charm rather than statuesque looks, with large dark eyes. Margaret's father was the Honourable Peter Kemble, one of the wealthiest and most prominent men in the colony of New Jersey, a staunch Tory, and who at the time was the presiding officer of the Royal Council of New Jersey.

By June 1764 the Gages had moved in to a double house on Broad Street surrounded by elegant gardens. Historians have commented disparagingly that the address was not especially exclusive. Their neighbours comprised a wigmaker and hairdresser opposite, and next to the tonsorial artists was the residence of Bernard Andrews, an "embroiderer".

For the next nine years the house became the centre of all British military activities in America, and were probably the happiest in the life of Thomas Gage. Professionally, he had risen almost to the top of the ladder. There must have also been satisfaction in the fact he administered the peace-time standing army in its far flung forts across half a continent. In addition the Gages were famous throughout the colonies for "conjugal felicity". They were enormously popular in New York social circles, and led society in style, fashion and the making of a new world. They entertained liberally; they met with all the distinguished visitors in the town including such persons as Lord William Campbell, Sir William Draper, the great Cherokee chiefs Attakullakulla and Ouconnostotah, James Otis and George Washington (though by this time, their relationship had begun to cool). Thomas was modest, diffident, good-natured, and generous, he believed in education, and his many children were sent "home" to school as soon as they were old enough to endure the voyage, where they were looked after by Thomas's brother, William Hall, the second Viscount and his wife, "Aunt Betsey", living at Firle Place.

Thomas Gage's finances steadily increased during his American service. As Commander in Chief he received a salary of £10 a day, no mean sum then. Further, he was given one hundred rations per day, which he did not draw, but for which the army paid him £2 10s. cash, together with approximately £164 for heating ("firing"). He was also paid the salary of a Colonel, since in theory he retained the command of one regiment or another from 1757, until his death. As colonel, he enjoyed further perquisites. From the 1760s onwards he was concerned for the future of his family – 11 children in total – and he purchased large amounts of land with the prospect that their value would increase as the colonies developed. In 1765 through the assistance of Governor Montague Wilmot of Nova Scotia where he was given a Canadian grant on the St. John River, upon which Gagetown, New Brunswick now stands. In October 1765 Gage purchased 18,000 acres for £100, located in what is now Oneida county, New York State. He also acquired a plantation in Montserrat, West Indies that brought in an income of £600 a year. Under the system of primogeniture, Gage would not have had these opportunities in England. Therefore by 1774, Thomas had acquired a strong stake in America and the Empire: he wanted to keep the peace. He worked faithfully to support the King and Parliament, at the same time as seeking to bring about harmony with the Americans. Even his enemies regarded him as decent, able and full of good intentions, referring to him as *a good and wise man …. surrounded with difficulties.* In America, Thomas was especially proud of the discipline of his forces and always insisted that his troops were bound by "constitutional laws" and permitted them to "do nothing but what is strictly legal", even when severely provoked. He recognized an obligation to respect what he called "the common rights of mankind". Equally, he also saw the need for strict authority and decisive action if the empire was to be preserved. By temperament and principle, Gage was an ethical and conservative person, with an infinite capacity for taking pains. His moderation grew stronger as his responsibilities increased.

When Gage moved to New York to become Commander in Chief in 1763 his responsibilities were enormous. He was given five thousand men to hold fast for England the whole eastern half of North America. He had to preserve a vast domain from danger whether from Spanish attack, an attempt by the French to rebuild their empire, Indian uprisings, or rebellion by Britain's own colonists. No attempt had been made by the British government to establish a civil government. Gage's skills as a conciliator were well used and one of his most significant contributions was the fact that peace between the British and Indians reigned everywhere by the end of 1765.

In 1763, the British politicians were concerned with the problem of governing an enormous empire. They recognised the need for maintaining a standing army of British regulars in America to garrison the new possessions. However, never had such a large force been stationed in America in peacetime. The national debt in Britain was at an all time high, £130,000,000, a staggering sum in those days, taxes were onerous, and it was the general perception that as the colonists had benefited richly from the expenditures of the Mother Country, why should the Americans not carry some of the burden of the cost in future? This resulted in the Stamp Act crisis and its repeal. Gage saw the need to provide finance to support the costs of maintaining forces in America, and yet the Stamp Act in 1765 completely took him by surprise, he wrote home to a minister in London, *I must confess to you, Sir, that during the commotions in North America, I have never been more at a loss how to act.* This was to be Gage's first real brush with mob rebuttal.

Following the Boston Massacre on March 5, 1770, Thomas took a different view of the colonial problem. He decided that the prevailing tensions rose from a deeper root, specifically in the growth of what he called democracy. As early as 1772, he wrote to his superiors in London, *Democracy is too prevalent in America, and claims the greatest attention to prevent its increase.* A large part of the problem, he was convinced arose from the vast abundance of cheap land in America – precluded in England under the system of primogeniture. Gage observed that, *the people themselves have gradually retired from the Coast* and *are, already, almost out of the reach of Law and Government.*

In April 1770 the British Government repealed the Townsend Acts, with the exception of the tax on tea. Three years of relative quiet began in the fall. As he had served nearly twenty years in America without vacation, Gage felt that he could apply for a leave of absence *because of affairs of my family which require my presence for some time in England.* Doubtless he wished to see his brother, and meet his sister in law; Margaret was eager to meet her husband's English relatives, and both of them would have been keen to visit their children in school. Besides it would be pleasant to take in the sights of London, enjoy the English countryside, to renew old friendships, and to learn what was current in British politics. Permission was finally granted and Thomas and Margaret went home, embarking upon Captain Effingham Lawrence's *Earl of Dunmore* on June 8, 1773, where he was greeted triumphantly.

Their departure was sincerely regretted, since it was very possible that General Gage might not return. The unequivocal esteem in which Gage was held, was clearly demonstrated at a dinner given in New York in his honour by the mayor and council, the day before the Gage's departure. By way of a token of the affection and respect in which Thomas was regarded, he was granted the Freedom of the City of New York. This gold Freedom Box is of extraordinary interest considering that gold work from the American colonies is extremely rare. The Freedom Box was initiated under the Mayor of New York, Whitehead Hicks. Minutes of a meeting of the city's Common Council on May 20, 1773 record, *Communicated to this Board that General Gage Intends shortly to leave this province for Europe, and that as his Conduct had been generally approved of by the Inhabitants of this City, therefore proposed that this Board Should Address him & the same time prefer him with the freedom of this Corporation, the seal whereof to be Enclosed in a Gold Box. This Board therefore agreeing in Sentiment with Mr. Mayor ORDER'D that an Address & freedom be prepared Accordingly.* The Freedom Document stills hangs at Firle Place, the Gage family ancestral home in Sussex, England.

After the Boston Tea Party on December 16, 1773 Thomas Gage was sent back to America as the best man to control the situation. He was also made Governor of Massachusetts, replacing Thomas Hutchinson, arrived in Boston aboard Captain Bishop's H.M.S. *Liveley* on May 13, 1774. Margaret followed later, initially spending some time with her family in New York. Finally she left for Boston under the escort of Major Shirreff, arriving there on September 12.

She found her husband virtually besieged. Parliament had responded to the Tea Party with great and misdirected energy by instituting forceful measures, a series of laws called "The Coercive Acts", and as already mentioned were dubbed the "Intolerable Acts" by the colonists. The port of Boston was declared closed to all trade and the Royal Navy was dispatched to ensure that no ships sailed in or out of the harbour. Over two hundred years after the event, it is easy to see that the Boston Port Bill and the demand of the British Government that payment be made for the ruined teas, was a stupid measure. Parliament also endeavoured to limit the power of popular institutions and increase executive power. Henceforth, the Royal Governor, not the assembly would choose members of the Council. Gatherings where, *the very dregs of the people* frustrating the will of Parliament were outlawed. As Governor, Thomas Gage came to proclaim the solemn league and covenant as a traitorous assemblage, proclaimed as for *the encouragement of virtue and the suppression of vice*. While these were measures aimed at diffusing resistance, they instead provoked outrage and offence.

General Gage's tenure in Boston was unappreciated at home: his forces were both insufficient, ill-supplied and demoralised, he lacked the authority to deal with constant irritations such as basic powers of arrest, tensions were increasing as a result of the Army's practice of placing troops in private homes or 'quartering' for lack of barracks, especially in Boston, and in his day to day existence he found himself in a viper's nest of spies.

In March 1774 if Gage really believed that he could police Boston with four regiments, on his return to Boston by the end of August he had no illusions. He realized the situation was grave. Gage constantly pressed for reinforcements. In a private letter to Viscount Barrington dated November 2nd he wrote … *if you resist and not yield [to American demands], that resistance should be effectual at the beginning. If you think ten thousand men sufficient, send twenty, if one million is thought enough, give two; you will save both blood and treasure in the end. A large force will terrify, and engage many to join you, a middling one will encourage resistance, and gain no friends. The crisis is indeed an alarming one, & Britain had never more need of wisdom, firmness, and union than at this juncture.*

By December when the colonists seized the arsenal in Fort William and Mary, Gage wrote home to Lord Dartmouth, the Colonial Secretary: *I hope you will send me a sufficient force to command the country … affairs are at a crisis and if you give way it is for ever.* His repeated requests were met with derision and scorn in London. Indeed, in November when Gage went further, and urged that the Coercive Acts should be suspended until more troops could be sent to Boston, the idea caused consternation in London. The King himself angrily rejected Gage's advice as *the most absurd that can be suggested.*

What did Thomas do, beyond making his military preparations to meet the crisis that arose in the late summer of 1774? He took great care not to force an armed clash; he reported the situation diligently to Barrington and Dartmouth in London; he displayed the prudence and coolness for which he was so well known; he was not only polite to delegations of Americans who sought him out, he was even gracious. He worked with the officials of Boston to prevent clashes between his men and the townspeople. This soldier who hated war did not wish to use force against the Americans, except as the last resort. If there was to be armed conflict, he would let the Americans or the British government instigate it.

General Gage was recalled to London in October 1775, on the pretext that he was required in England to help lay plans for major operations in 1776. Gage was never to return to America. When General Howe took over as Commander in Chief, this reflected a marked change in tenor and a significant watershed concerning the future of the colonies: the person who at heart had the greater interest to finding a peaceful and conciliatory way forward was replaced by those purely of a professional military mindset. The rest is history. Thomas died of bowel cancer at Portland Place on April 2, 1787 and was laid to rest quietly in the family crypt at St. Peter's, Firle.

I have endeavoured to describe the character of Thomas Gage set against the time and as a central figure in the procession of events that led to American independence. Undoubtedly, Gage made tactical errors and lacked judgment in many aspects. He was in an invidious position, compounded by his own personal shortcomings. Thomas was often too scrupulous and cautious, so that events caught up with him, I suspect many of his attitudes were dictated by the fact he was a product of the English upper class system, which would have then been even more endemic in determining his mind-set: fundamentally he would have expected to be obeyed. Gage never curtailed the propagandists in Boston, whose seditious publications undermined moral and spread unrest through the colonies. Likewise his dispatches on Bunker Hill arrived in London two weeks after reports had purposely been sent ahead by the colonists, so that his own account was mis-read, no fault was accorded to the Government, and he was publicly discredited.

This was a time of great personal anguish both for Thomas and for Margaret. At the early stages of his administration Gage had vested enormous resourcefulness and belief into the making of the New World, and establishing stability, security and prosperity for the colonies. He owned land in North America, he had spent the majority of his life there – and indeed was very disillusioned and out of place when he returned briefly to England for a leave of absence in 1773. He wrote to a friend that London seemed as strange to him as Constantinople, or *any other city I have never seen*. By marriage he had relatives and friends there, most of his children were born in the north American continent: in short his life was America.

Following the American victory at Yorktown in 1776, Lord North fell from power and Gage's enemies were forced to resign from the British Cabinet in 1782. Thomas was subsequently promoted to a full General for his services in the colonies, together with recognition of the fact that his recommendations for sufficient reinforcements had never been heeded. It appears that Thomas continued to be held with affection in America. This may be demonstrated by the fact he was allowed to retain his land in New York State when most Loyalist properties were confiscated. According to General Gage's bank statements still held by Lloyds Bank in London, even though he had retired from Boston, he continued to collect £1,500 a year as Governor of Massachusetts. His absence was looked upon as temporary. Likewise, Gage's name remained on the rolls of the celebrated American Philosophical Society of Philadelphia, of which he became a member on December 20, 1768, until his death.

Effectively, Thomas Gage was a victim of circumstance: in the wrong place at the wrong time. This became evidently clear to me when my cousin, the eighth Viscount Gage and head of the family, and myself were invited to participate in the re-enactment of the 225th anniversary of the skirmishes of Lexington and Concord, in April 2000. Many of the re-enactors were historians, so there proved to be a serious aspect to this experience. Consequently, I became the more focused upon the fact that the corollary of primogeniture – not so much taxation – was the underlying and most compellingly emotive and divisive issue that led the colonial quarrel into armed rebellion. The Quebec Act of 1774 effectively curtailed the availability of land in the context of the New World land rush. Now, not even the British government could stand in the way of an unstoppable westward train under a full head of steam. No wonder those young men streamed out on Lexington Common early in the morning of April 19, 1774, willing to risk their lives for their stake to land – that would have been unattainable to them, back in England. That evening we sat in General Gage's pew in the Anglican Old North End Church, Boston for a celebratory service. The church was lit by candlelight, music was provided by the fife and drum. Also seated in the congregation were the descendants of Samuel Adams and Paul Revere. It was a moving moment: we happily introduced ourselves and shook hands!

Bibliography:

Alden, John Richard, *General Gage in America: Being Principally a History of His Role in the American Revolution*, 1948, Louisiana State University

Fischer, David Hacket, *Paul Revere's Ride*, 1994, Oxford University Press

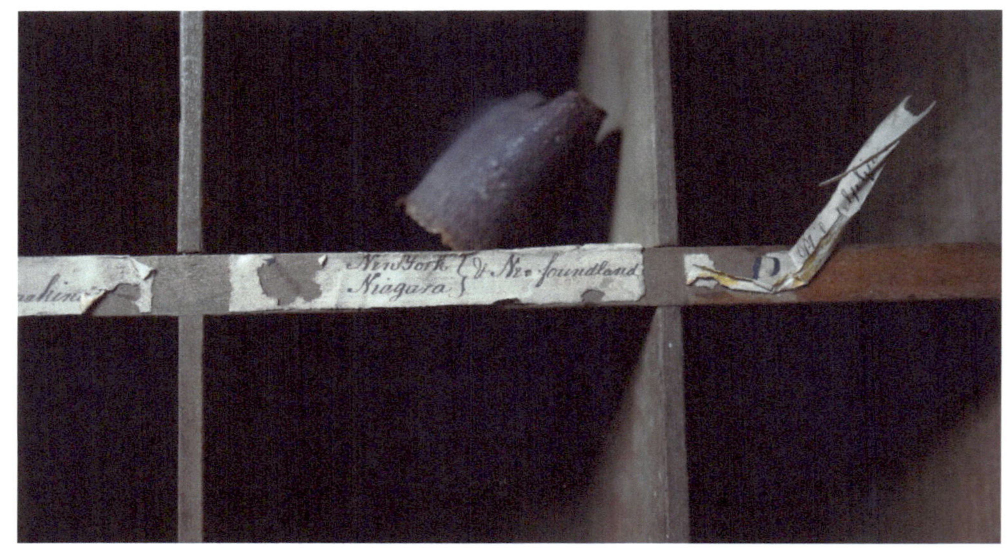

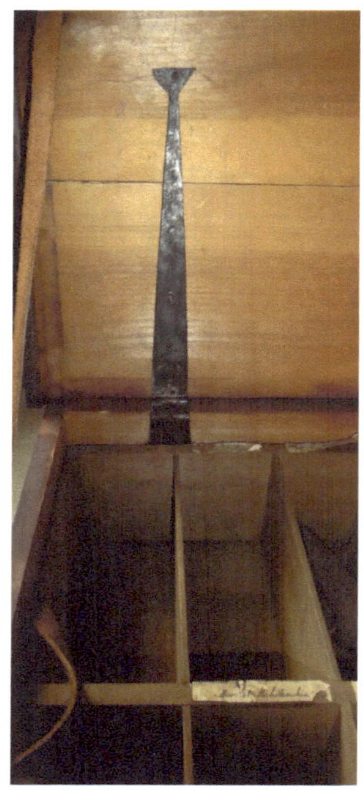

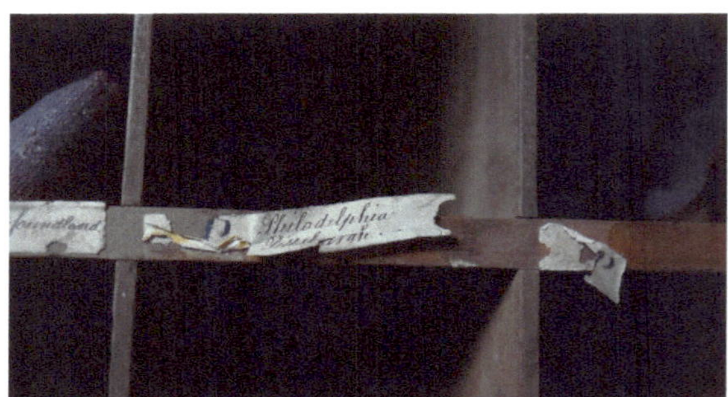

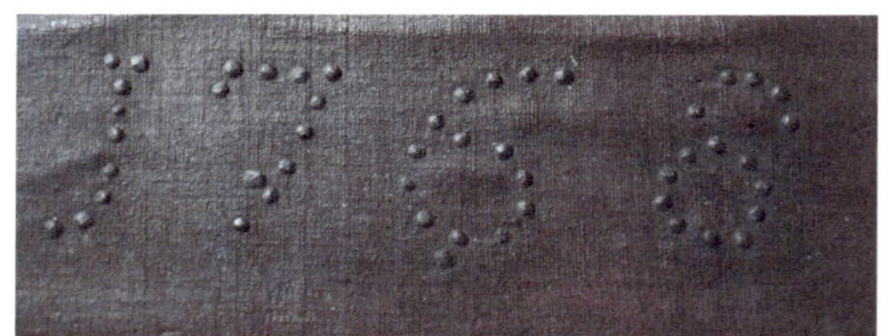

The Document Chest can be seen at Firle Place

General Gage by Deborah Gage

General Gage's Document Chest

Deborah Gage

Each year, Lieut. General Thomas Gage's correspondence was tied up together with red tape, according to city, and then filed within a pine chest, covered in hessian, and stained maroon-red, labelled with tack work for each year, this chest is inscribed with iron nail studs : 'SECTY OFF/No 5/ 1768' When he sailed home to England at the end of 1775, he took with him twelve of these chests, marking his term as Commander in Chief of the British forces in the North American colonies. They contained more than 21,000 manuscripts, now housed at the William L. Clements Library in Ann Arbour, Michigan. From his headquarters in New York, General Gage administered the peace-time standing army in its far-flung forts along the frontiers of the Colonies. This correspondence between various post commandants, colonial governors, the Indian superintendents, and cabinet ministers in England, together with copies of his replies, provide a complete dovetailed record of his tenure in North American, following the Seven Years War

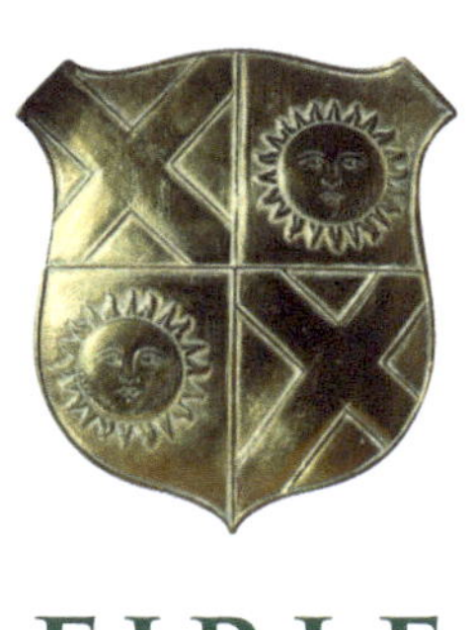

FIRLE

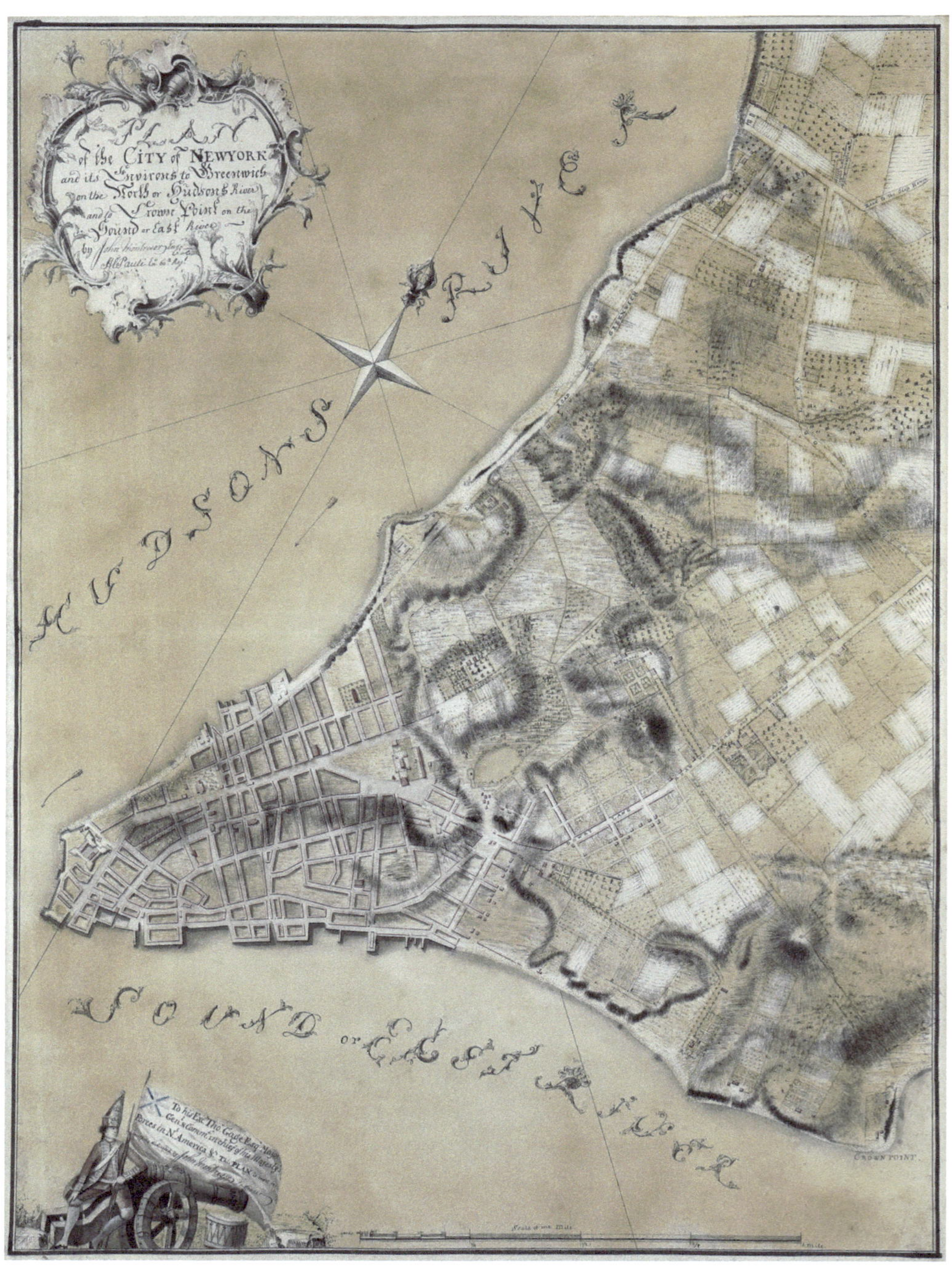

The 1766 Gage-Montresor 'fair draft' plan of the city of New York and its environs
Ink and wash on paper. Dedicated by Col. John Montresor (1736-1799) to
General Thomas Gage (1721-1787) On show at FIrle Place.

    General Gage by Deborah Gage

The Montresor Map of New York 1766

Deborah Gage

Fearing that Manhattan would soon become a battleground, on December 7, 1765 Thomas Gage summoned the best engineer on his staff, Lieutenant John Montresor, to survey and draw a map which would include all features pertinent to military manoeuvres.

Not only did the map need to be undertaken quickly, it would have to be undertaken in secrecy in order to avoid detection. The map, dated 1766 is a fascinating historical document not only because of what Montresor included – but also what he omitted. Main thoroughfares, fortifications and hilly terrain are shown while most street names, property boundaries and pertinent municipal buildings are virtually ignored.

The map makes it clear that General Gage's instructions were well understood: Montresor included only information relevant to military operations. As a result, this spare – yet elegant – map is a true testament to the turbulent times from which is was born.

In early 1766 Parliament repealed the Stamp Act, tension in the city subsided, Gage had no need to resort to military force. The map, also stands as very personal tribute: it is both dedicated to the General, while in the terrain beyond the tip of Manhattan, Montresor indicates a number of homes with the names of the owners who would have been related to his American-born wife, Margaret Kemble, of New Jersey. When both men retired to England in the later 1770s, they lived a few doors away from each other in Portland Place, London.

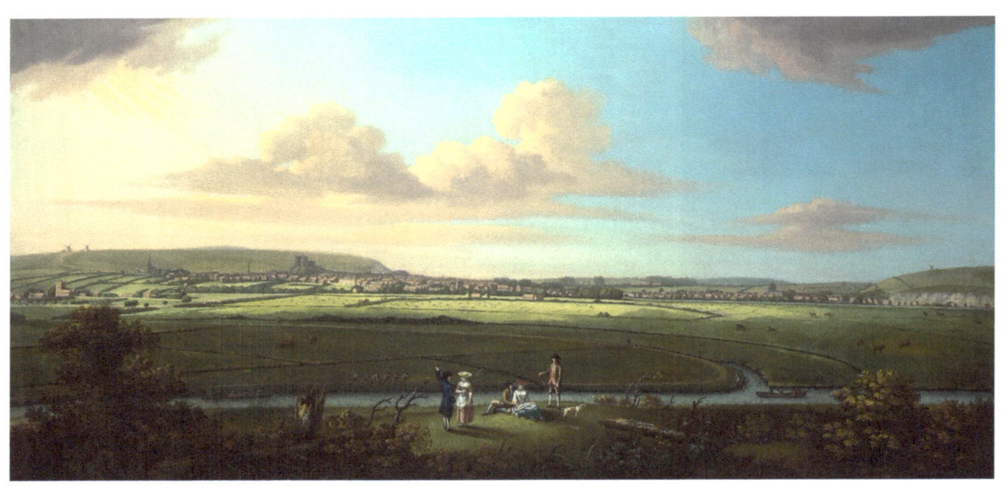

Dominic Serres, RA
Auch, Gascony 1719 – 1793 London
A panoramic view of Lewes, Sussex from the south-east, with gentlemen chatting to haymakers and men pulling a barge along the River Ouse. Signed and dated lower left: D. Serres .1760. Canvas: 35 3/8 x 71 5/8 in
Private collection, Sussex; photograph courtesy of Richard Green and p/c Sussex

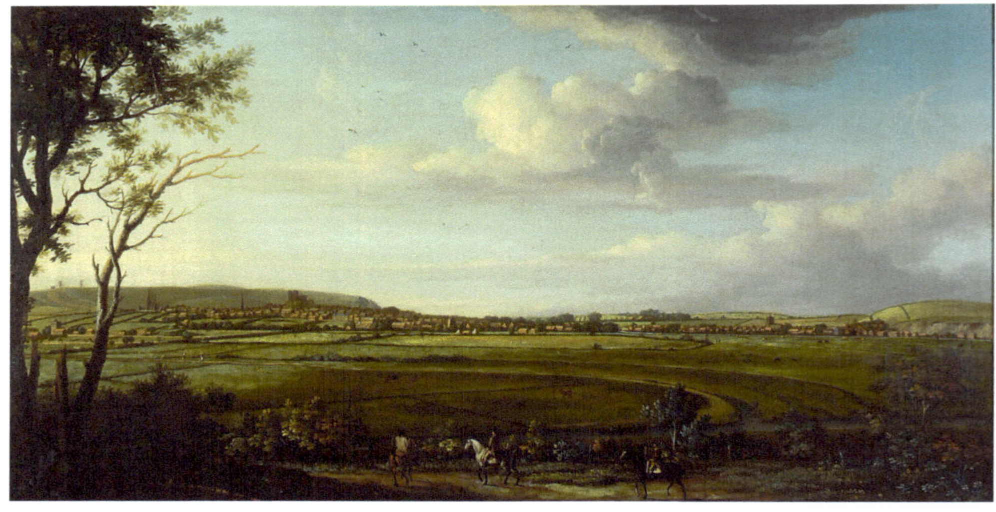

DOMINIC SERRES, RA
Auch, Gascony 1719 – 1793 London
A panoramic view of Lewes, Sussex from the south-east, with gentlemen on horseback admiring the view and men rowing a barge along the River Ouse Signed and dated centre left D. Serres. 1768. Canvas 25 ½ x 47 ½ in
Courtesy of Firle Place Preservation Trust

   Landscapes Of Lewes by Susan Morris

Description and Provenenace of the Landscapes of Lewes by Dominic Serres

Susan Morris

Editor's note: The first painting, shown opposite above, was executed in 1760, the second, shown below, in 1768, the year that Thomas Paine arrived in Lewes. They show some features changing over eight years, some of the changes due to a change of patronage. The second painting with less windmills and no shaft of sunlight on Pelham House. The 1760 painting is the much larger painting of the two, measuring 1.8 meters wide 0.9 metres high, the 1768 painting 1.2 metres wide 0.6 metres high.

Dominic Serres made a career as a marine painter but was also a fine landscapist, as this view of Lewes amply demonstrates. Dated 1760, it was made around the time that Serres moved his studio from London Bridge to Piccadilly, the heart of the fashionable West End. It was probably commissioned by Henry Shelley (1727-1805), mercer, moneylender and a leading citizen of Lewes, whose family had inhabited The Vine, St Anne's Hill (today Shelley's Hotel) since 1663.

The view is taken from the south-east, near the road from Southerham to Glynde, on land belonging to Lord Gage. In the foreground, gentlemen chat with haymakers and men pull a barge along the River Ouse. Near the junction of the Ouse and the Cockshut stream is a rowing boat. In the distance, beyond the green meadows with haymakers, is Lewes at the height of its Georgian prosperity. Lewes has been the de facto capital of East Sussex since medieval times, when the navigable Ouse made it a busy port.

A number of the handsome eighteenth century mansions which still distinguish the High Street can be made out, as well as the historic features which drew many eighteenth and nineteenth century antiquarians to write about the town. From left to right are the churches of St John's in Southover, St Anne's, St Michael's, All Saints and St Thomas in the Cliffe. Towering over Lewes is the Castle, raised by the feudal lord William de Warenne shortly after the Norman Conquest to defend the vital links between London and Normandy. Warenne and his wife Gundrada founded the Cluniac Priory of St Pancras whose grounds, including the Priory Mount to the left of Serres's painting, stretch towards the river. Other landmarks are the Tudor Westgate (left of St Michael's), the bridge spanning the Ouse at the eastern end of the High Street and the windmills on the Downs: Spittle and Town Mill to the left, Cliffe Mill to the right. The Ouse curves round the meadows and runs in a gleaming band just in front of the houses of Cliffe on the eastern side of the bridge.

Bands of sunlight and shadow enliven the panoramic landscape and evoke the breezy, changeable atmosphere of the Sussex Downs. A band of brilliant sunlight falls on Pelham House, acquired by the Whig MP Thomas Pelham of Catsfield in 1725. The Pelhams, headed by the wily statesman Thomas Pelham-Holles, 1st Duke of Newcastle (1693-1768), were the most influential political family in Lewes. The sunlight of their favour had fallen on the Shelleys: Henry Shelley (1693-1735), father of the Henry who commissioned this picture, had made his fortune as a mercer and moneylender to the Duke of Newcastle. Family prosperity allowed Henry Jnr to remodel The Vine in 1763, and Serres's painting no doubt hung in pride of place there. The painting remained with Shelley descendants until it was sold at Christie's in 1928, along with a smaller (25 ½ x 47 ½ in) painting of Lewes by Dominic Serres, signed and dated 1768, which is now in the collection of Viscount Gage at Firle Place.

Provenance:

The first painting probably commissioned by Henry Shelley (1727-1805), The Vine, St Anne's Hill, Lewes; his son Henry Shelley (1767-1811); by inheritance to his sister Cordelia Shelley (d.1854); her nephew Major George Charles Dalbiac (d.1888; son of Eleanor Shelley, who married in 1806 George John Dalbiac); his widow Caroline D'Albiac, 62 Denmark Villas,

Thomas Paine in Lewes 1768 - 1774

Hove, Sussex; her deceased sale, Christie's London, 2nd March 1928, lot 31 (sold for 95 gns) Major-General James Renton, Rowfold Grange, Billingshurst; his daughter Mrs Kathleen Vickers Exhibited: 1977-2003 on loan to Barbican House Museum, Lewes Castle, Lewes . The smaller replica was commissioned by the lawyer and antiquarian John Elliott (1724-1782), a friend of Henry Shelley, who left Henry the painting in his will, no doubt as a memorial of their shared interest in Lewes's history. Serres's 1768 receipt from Elliott survives in the Elliott papers at the Barbican House Museum. The painting differs from the 1760 version by the addition of a repoussoir of trees at the left and three gentlemen riders instead of the gentlemen chatting to haymakers in the larger work.

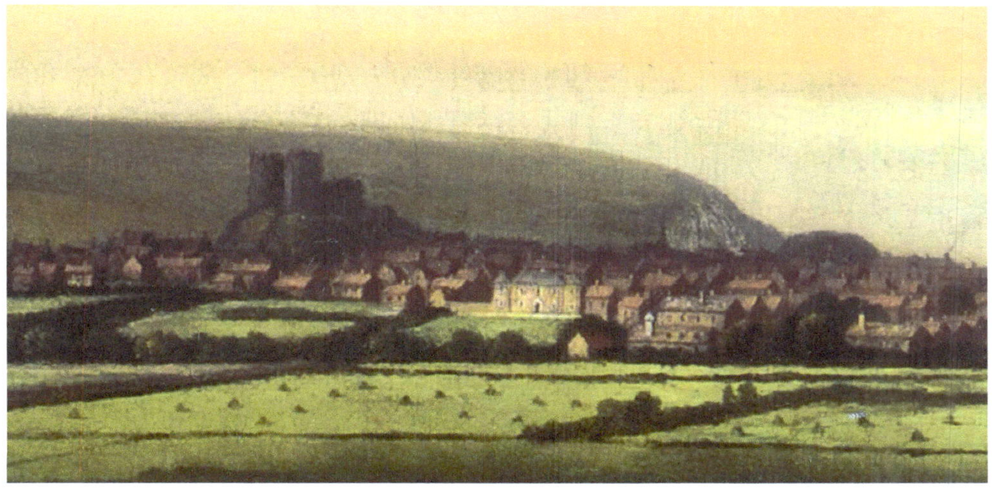

D. Serres 1760 detail
Shaft of light illuminating Pelham
House

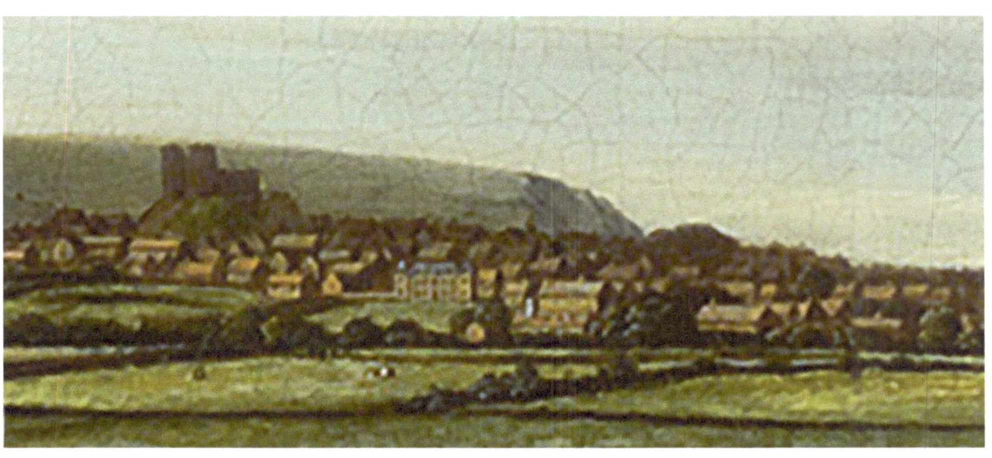

D. Serres 1768 detail
Pelham House not illuminated

Dominic Serres, although French, was the most successful London-domiciled painter of naval actions of the Seven Years' War (1756-63) and the War of American Independence (1775-83). Serres came from the Gascon gentry; his uncle was Archbishop of Rheims and in his Gentleman's Magazine obituary he is referred to as Comte Serres. He was educated at the English Benedictine school at Douai, which explains his ease among the English.

Intended by his family for the priesthood, Serres ran away to sea. He was captured and brought to England, possibly late in the War of the Austrian Succession (1741-48). Serres's charm, education and practical knowledge of seamanship proved most useful in gaining patrons when he decided to make his living as a painter. His early works, influenced by Charles Brooking, are luminous calms with a romantic air; later he took a more realistic approach to his subjects, which make his paintings valuable historical documents. Serres was a founder member of the Royal Academy in 1768 and its librarian in the last year of his life; from 1779 he was Marine Painter to George III. He exhibited at the Free Society exhibitions and became a member of the Incorporated Society of Artists in 1765. Dominic Serres died in London in 1793. His two sons, Dominic the Younger (c.1761/2-c.1804) and John Thomas (1759-1825) also became marine painters.

I am grateful to Chris Milburn, Emma O'Connor and John Bleach of the Barbican House Museum for their invaluable information about the history of Lewes.

Bibliography

Alan Russett, Dominic Serres RA: John Farrant, Sussex Depicted, Sussex Record Society vol. 85, 2001, p.29

Landscapes Of Lewes by Susan Morris

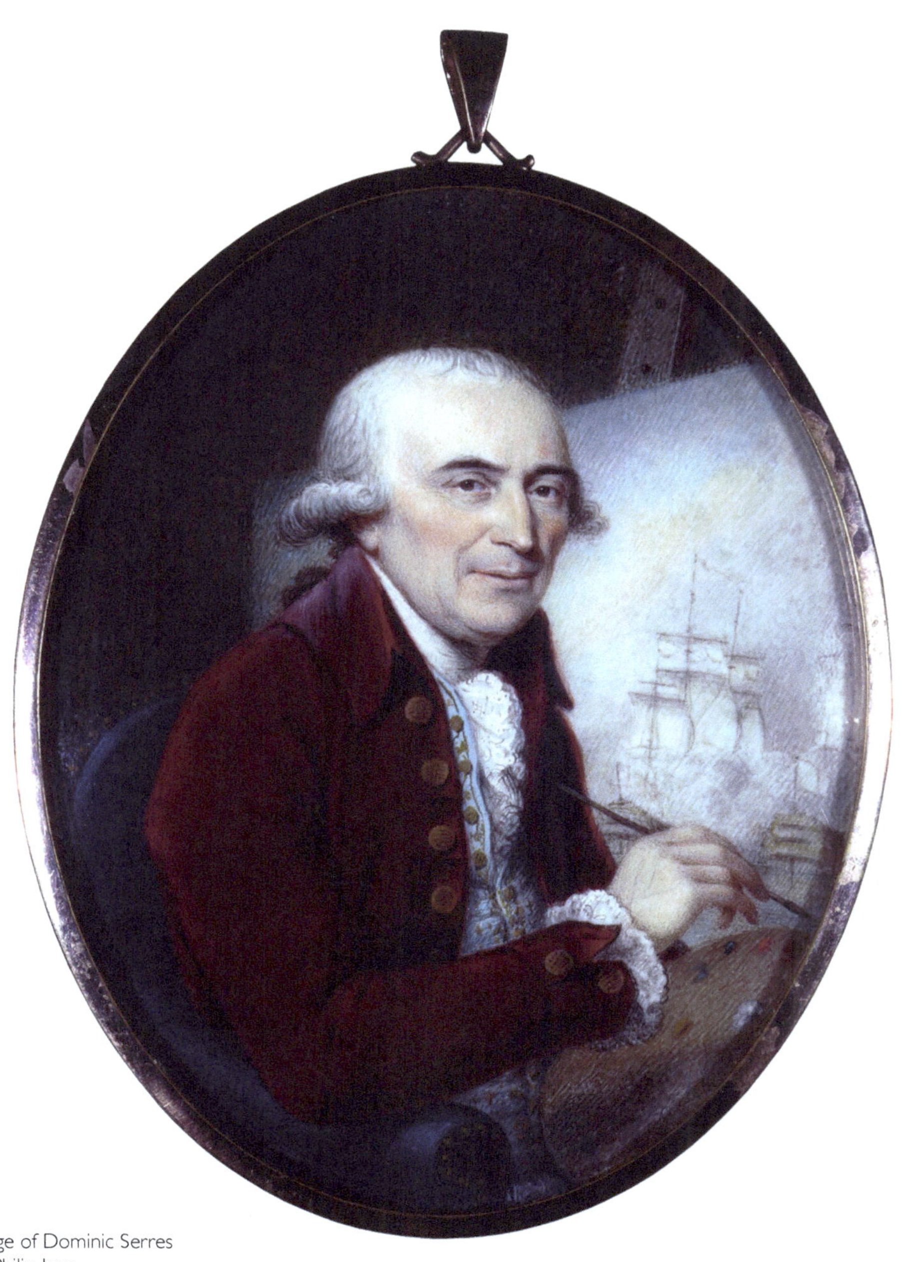

Image of Dominic Serres
By Philip Jean
Watercolour and bodycolour
on ivory, 1788 © National
Portrait Gallery

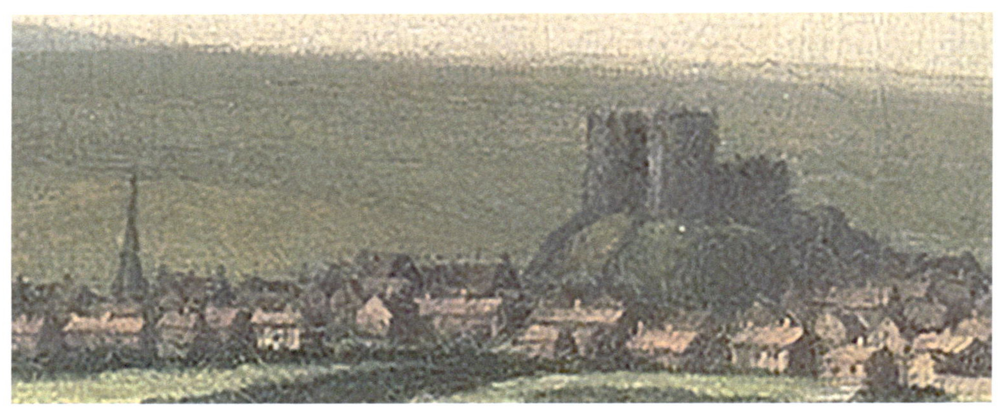

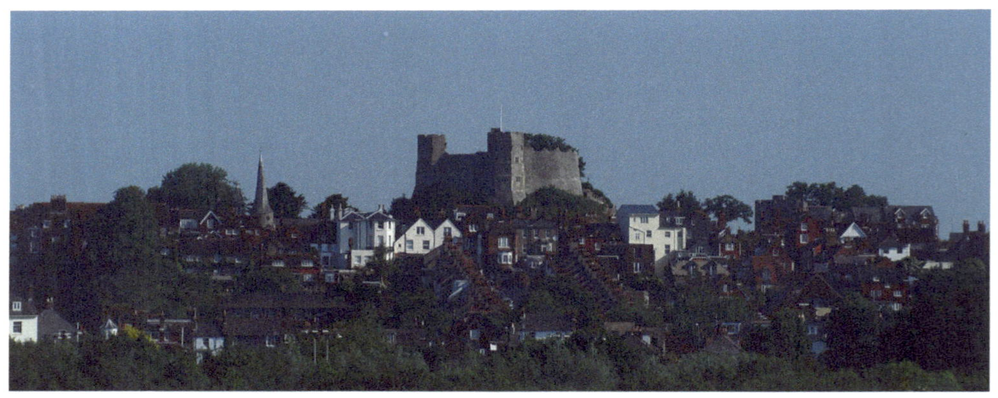

The Skyline of Lewes Castle, 1760 Serres and
today

 Landscapes Of Lewes by Susan Morris

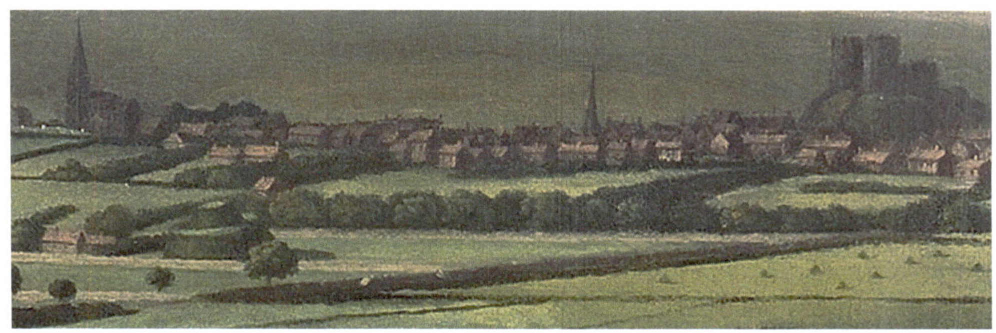

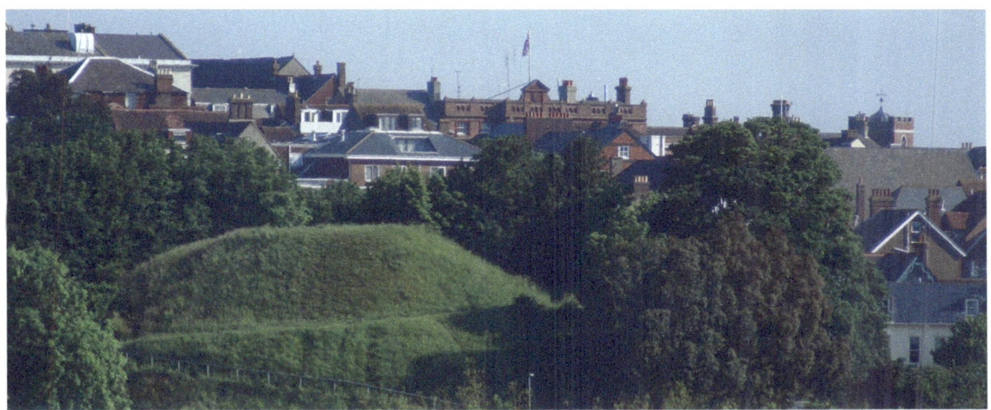

The Mound 1760 Serres and today, from left to right,
the Law Courts, the White Hart Hotel, Lewes Town
Hall (flagged) and the Market Tower in the background

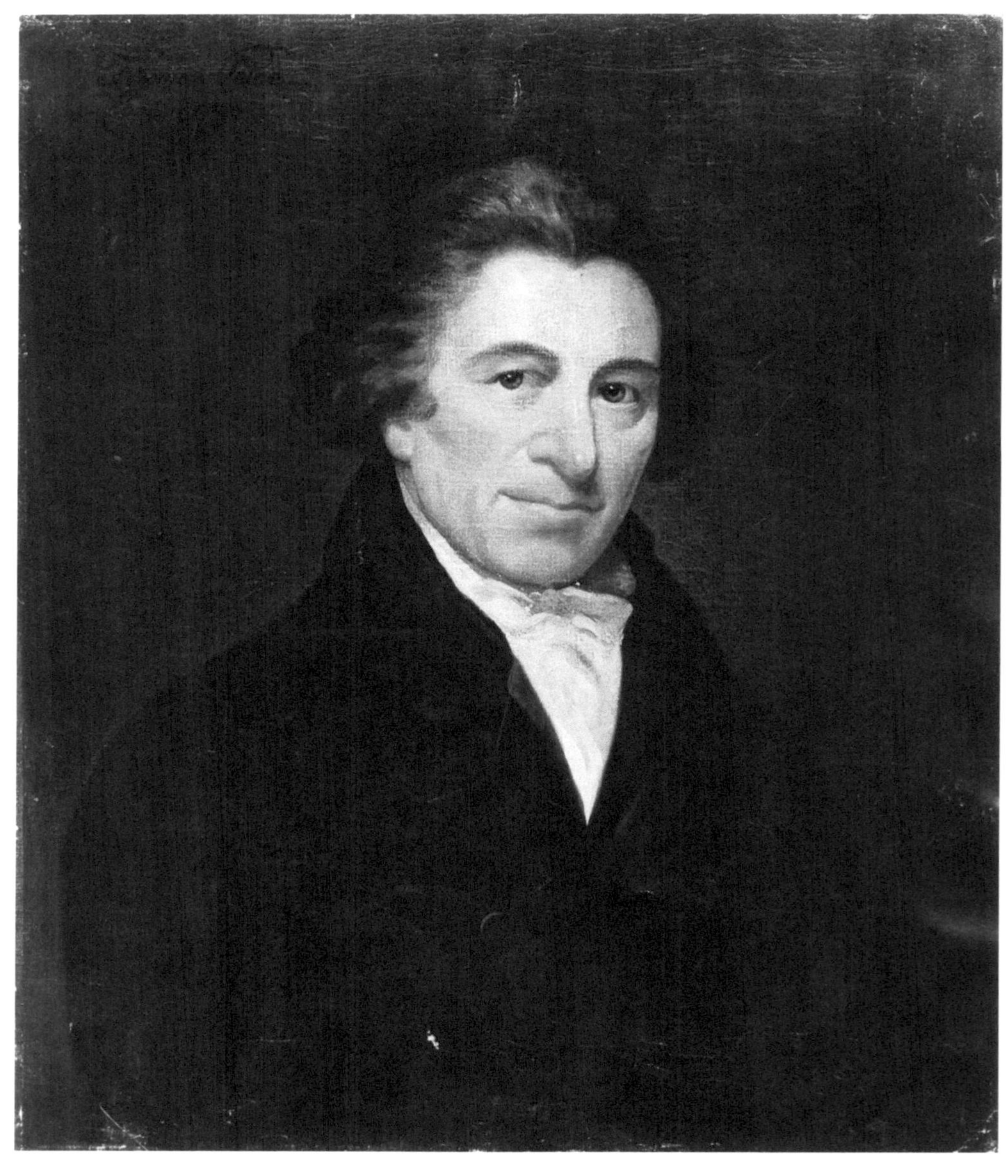

52   The 1790 Painting of Thomas Paine : Paul Myles

The Painting of Thomas Paine
1790 London

Paul Myles

This photographic image of a painting was found in the box dedicated to Thomas Paine in the Heinz Archive of the National Portrait Gallery (NPG) which was offered to the nation in the early 20th century but not purchased. The painting was sold by Sothebys on the 8th of May 1951 lot. 354, it may have left the country. It would be marvellous to see the real painting, and research the artist, unknown at the moment, using modern methods. A search for Thomas Paine on the NPG website revealed images that progressively depart from any likeness to a real person. The best image is an engraving by William Sharp circa 1876, after George Romney's oil on canvas 1792 which is now lost. The most commonly used image is a painting by Milliere, after Sharp, which has very fleshy dark tones. A painting by Laurent Dabos in 1791 bears no real likeness to any other image of Paine, and subsequent images seem to depart further from realism and towards caricature. The John Kay etching sports a cartoon nose, and the James Gadby sketch seems to descend completely into farce.

After the decision to use the image opposite on the front of the first edition of this book, a curious event happened. I received a phone call from an individual who thought that they may be a descendent of Thomas Paine. Whilst it is known that there are no known direct descendants of Paine, I agreed to meet, and a visit to my house was arranged. I kept a lookout in anticipation, and when this person came up the steps to the house, a chill went through me. The likeness to the image opposite was astonishing. After two meetings we established beyond any reasonable doubt that this individual was descended from Paine's uncle, the brother of his father. This link to the past is perhaps the best proof of what Thomas Paine looked like in the prime of his life.

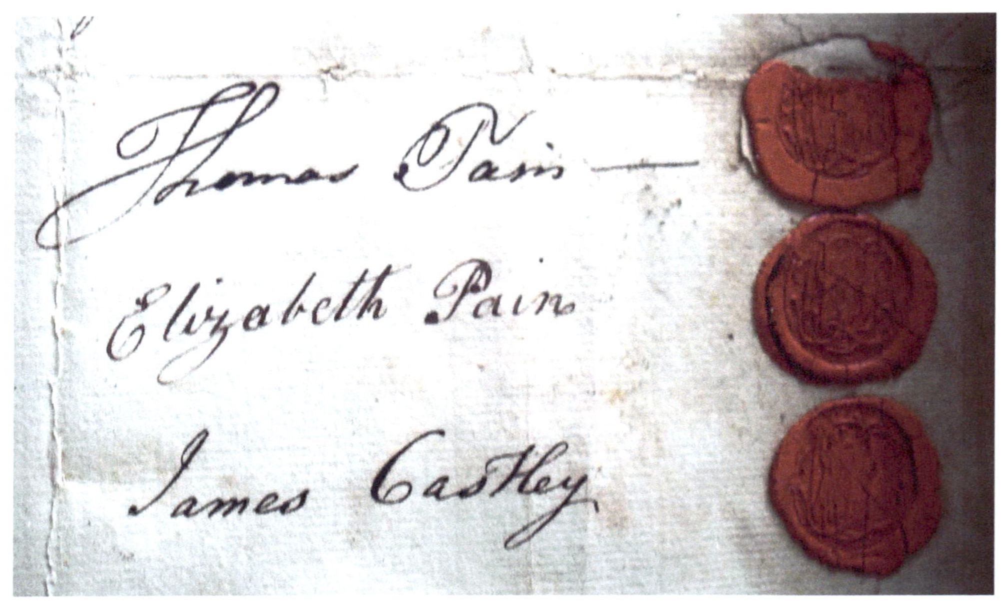

Details from the separation document
ESRO AMS 7000/1

          The Separation Document by Paul Myles

The Separation Document

Paul Myles

Towards the end of the Lewes Thomas Paine Festival in July 2009 I received a phone call from Cowfold in Sussex. The caller had in his possession a separation document between Thomas Paine and his wife Elizabeth. Martin Eidelberg, a visiting professor from New York, a specialist in documents and art from this period, came with me to see it. Martin confirmed it was the real thing, and we advised the owner to take it to Bonhams for sale by auction. The document was bought by East Sussex County Record Office under the careful eye of Christopher Whittick, the County Archivist, at a hammer price of £11,000, entirely funded by grants and donations.

Elizabeth Paine invoked the Canon Law doctrine, if it could be proved that a husband was incapable of performing his conjugal duty, the marriage was void *ab initio*, the marriage was never created nor valid to begin with. Clio Rickman, Paine's lifelong friend, and first friendly biographer, wrote:

That he did not cohabit with her from the moment they left the altar till the day of their separation, a space of three years, although they lived together, is an indubitable truth. It is also true, that no physical defect, on the part of Mr. Paine, can be adduced as a reason for such conduct. I have in my possession the letters and documents on this subject - Mr Francis Wheeler's letters from Lewes of April 16, 1774, to Mr Philip Moore, proctor in the Commons and his reply of April 18 1774; and from Dr. Manning of Lewes I have frequently heard a candid detail of the circumstances. Mr Paine's answer upon my once referring to this subject was " It is nobody's business but my own: I had cause for it, but I will name it to no one" This I can assert, that Mr. Paine always spoke tenderly and respectfully of his wife; and sent her several times pecuniary aid, without her knowing even whence it came.

Mr Wheeler was a solicitor in Lewes, Mr Moore was a proctor, the equivalent of a barrister, practising in the Ecclesiastical Courts; Doctors Commons was the equivalent of an Inn of Court for such lawyers. At this time divorce required an act of parliament, and then only for adultery. It could be afforded only by the very wealthy, women could not procure a divorce unless compounded by incest or bigamy. On average there was only two divorces granted per year in England in the 18th century.

Another biographer of Paine, Vale, wrote in 1841 about Elizabeth Paine after their separation:
She was afterward a professor of a sectarian religion in Cranbrook, Kent, and boarded in the house of a watchmaker, a member of the same church; his house was consequently visited by religious people, many of them with strong prejudices, and some very ignorant. These, after the publication of the "Age of Reason," would sometimes speak disrespectfully of Mr. Paine in her presence, when, she uniformly left the room without a word. If, too, she was questioned on the subject of their separation, she did the same. We have these facts from those who resided with her. Our most intimate friend at one period, was a Mr. Bourne, a watch maker in Rye, about eighteen miles from Cranbrook, England. This gentleman was apprenticed in the house where Mrs. Paine lived : he sat at the same table with her for years. We have these facts confirmed by other residents at Cranbrook. Thus nothing could be learned from her, except that though she differed from Mr. Paine on religious subjects, she could not bear to hear him spoken ill of.

The house that Elizabeth boarded in was that of her brother, Thomas Ollive, a clockmaker. He was a fiercely religious man who, apart from the general attacks on Paine promulgated from the government, would have reacted badly to Paine's later attack on organised religion, *Age of Reason.*

Judith Brent and I transcribed the document in 2009. Some key parts of it will be discussed below; it begins:

Articles of Agreement Tripartite Indented had made and agreed upon the Fourth day of June in the Year of our Lord One thousand and Seven Hundred and Seventy four Between Thomas Pain of Lewes in the County of Sussex [late- inserted above] Excise Officer of the first part Elizabeth Pain Wife of the said Thomas Pain (late Elizabeth Ollive Spinster) of the Second part and the Reverend James Castley of Lewes aforesaid Clerk of the Third part.

Tripartite means that it was repeated, copied, three times on one long manuscript, each copy being given to each party, Thomas Paine, Elizabeth Paine and James Castley. The cut was made with a wavy edge to ensure that each part was genuine. The actual separation document fell out of a book by Smollet. It was found in a cellar of a jeweller's shop in Hastings. The manager of the shop had an interest in old books and there were some just lying in the cellar. The Smollet was a version that was printed for the American market originally, which tantalisingly means it could have returned from America, possibly Paine's copy.

Whereas certain unhappy Quarrels and dissensions have arisen (and which do now in part subsist) between the said Thomas Pain and Elizabeth his Wife for putting an End to which They the said Thomas Pain and Elizabeth his Wife hath mutually agreed to live separate and apart.

The unhappy quarrels must have abated, proved by the statement that *they in part subsist.*

And whereas Samuel Olive late of Lewes aforesaid Grocer deceased Father of the said Elizabeth in and by his last Will and Testament Did give and Devise All that his Messuage or Tenement and Appurtenances wherein he lived Situate in the parish of Saint Michaels in the Town of Lewes aforesaid unto his Wife Hester Olive for and during the Term of her Natural Life and after her Decease he gave and Devised the same unto John Ridge of Kingston in the said County Gentleman and John Attersoll of Lewes aforesaid Carpenter and the Survivor of them and the Heirs and Assigns of the Survivor In Trust to sell the same and out of the Monies arising thereby In Trust to divide the same between his Four Children John Samuel Thomas and Elizabeth (now the Wife of the said Thomas Pain as aforesaid) in equal shares and in case any or either of them should happen to Die before the Monies Should become Payable then to pay the same in such manner as therein is mentioned

As in and by the said Will and Probate thereof relation being thereunto had more fully will appear Now the said Thomas Pain hath also consented and agreed that the said Elizabeth shall have and take her share of the said Monies of the said House when the same shall become due and Payable and will also give any Discharge that shall be then required to and for the Use of the said Elizabeth

Thomas Paine could have held out for all Elizabeth's entire inheritance. Marriage at that time meant all that belonged to Elizabeth became the property of the husband. Unusually for the time having provided for his wife's need for her life, Elizabeth's father had left all his wealth in equal shares to his four children male and female alike.

     The Separation Document by Paul Myles

And the said Elizabeth hath agreed to give up to the said Thomas Pain the sum of [Forty Five Pounds - *inserted*] now in her Possession on or before the [Sixth - *inserted*] day of [June - *inserted*]

This was a significant sum of money. Paine had just produced a pamphlet arguing for better pay and conditions for his fellow officers of excise, citing an annual salary of £50 per annum, reduced to £32 after tax, expenses and the costs of keeping a horse were deducted. The sum of £45 in a single payment represented well over a year's salary for Thomas Paine. This must have played an important part in his new start in the North American Colonies, and it meant he could enter the next phase of his life with confidence. It was also a significant enough sum for Paine to relinquish the rights afforded to him by marriage. Below are the remaining key points from the document:

James Castley indemnified Thomas Paine against any claims for maintenance by Elizabeth and the liability for any contracts entered into by her.

Thomas to allow Elizabeth to live apart and follow any trade or business as though she were a femme sole, and not take action against her in the ecclesiastical court or any other court, nor visit her without her consent.

Thomas not to slander or defame Elizabeth, detract from her good character or do any injury whatsoever to her reputation.

Elizabeth may take 'a few fixtures' remaining in their late dwelling house at Lewes, valued by Mr Verrall at about 25 shillings

All parties made the best of a difficult situation. Thomas Paine sent Elizabeth money from time to time, and Elizabeth would not speak ill of her husband. Whilst the world raged around them, there was a lifelong calm between these two after the initial trouble. Elizabeth was buried in Cranbrook graveyard by her married name, where it can be seen to this day, near to her brother Thomas.

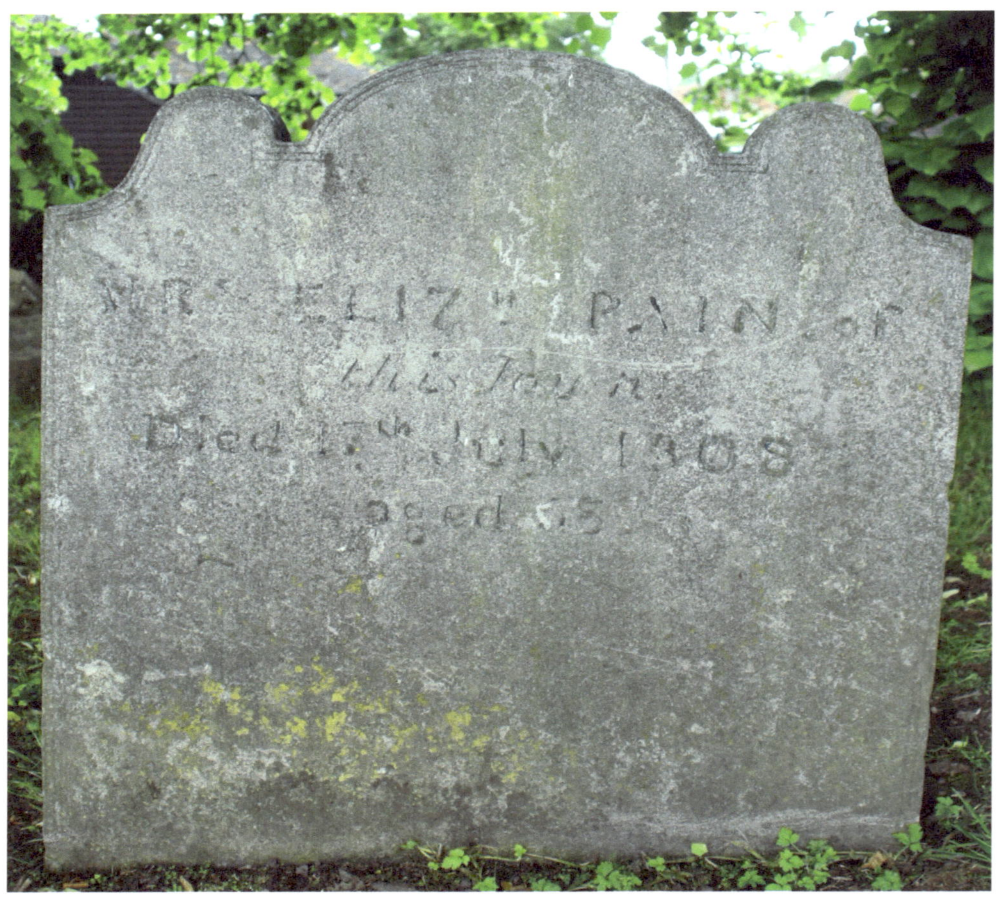

Mrs ELIZ^H PAIN *of*
this Town
Died 17 th July 1808
aged 58

                    The Separation Document by Paul Myles

Thomas Paine in Lewes 1768 - 1774

Bibliography:

A McLaren: *Impotence A Cultural History*. University of Chicago Press 2007

East Sussex Record Office: *Separation agreement between Thomas Pain [Paine] of Lewes, late excise officer, and his wife Elizabeth, née Olive Date: 1774* Repository reference: AMS 7000

C Rumsey: *The Wife of a Revolutionary* TPS Bulletin No.2. Vol.4. 1999 Thomas Paine Society

East Sussex Record Office: *Transcript of AMS (Separation Agreement) 7000/1 by Judith Brent and Paul Myles* 2009 Repository reference: AMS 7000/2

G. Vale : *The Life of Thomas Paine* New York 1853

Sybil Wolfram: 'Divorce in England' *1700-1857 Oxford Journal of Legal Studies*, Vol. 5, No. 2 (Summer, 1985), pp. 155-186 Published by: Oxford University Press

T. Clio Rickman: *The Life of Thomas Paine*. London, 1819

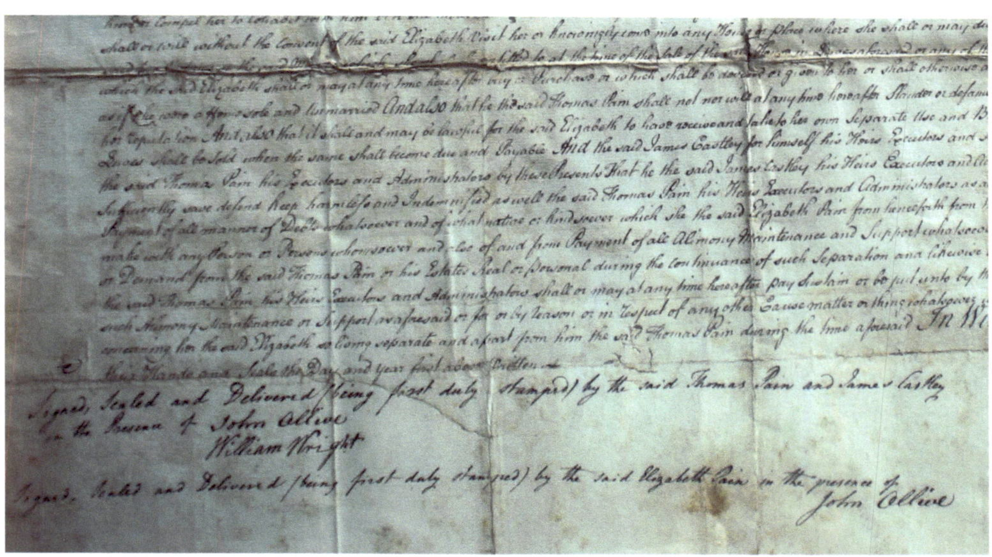

Detail from the separation document
ESRO AMS 7000/1

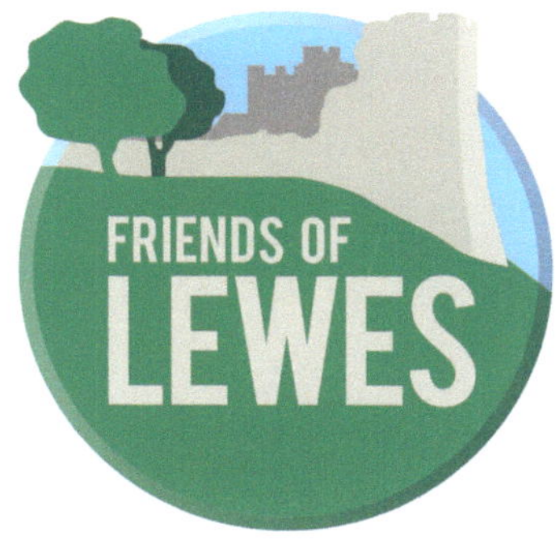

friends-of-lewes.org.uk

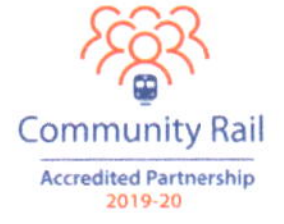

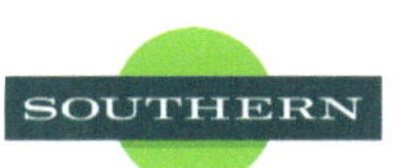

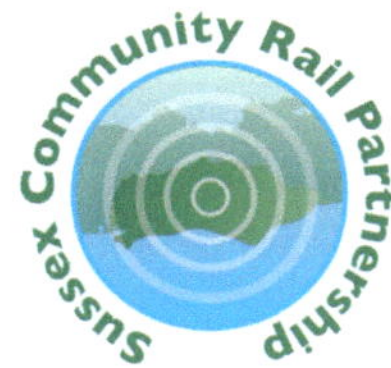

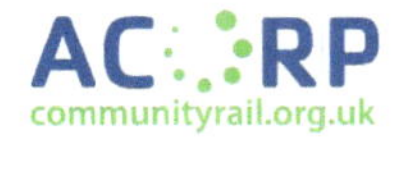

THE
CHALK
CLIFF
TRUST

Postscript

Paul Myles

*T*his second edition was a welcome opportunity to include the Separation Document and more information about General Thomas Gage. The Montresor Map of New York, the Document Chest and also the document granting Thomas Gage the Freedom of the City of New York presented on June 7, 1773 can all be seen at Firle Place, see www.firle.com for opening times.

For further reading about Thomas Paine read *The Rise of Thomas Paine,* published by the Thomas Paine Society UK in 2018. After some 7 years of intermittent research, I found some of the missing signatures from the petition of 3000 officers of excise in the treasury boxes at the National Archive. Not catalogued, it was a very exciting find. The signatures, the way that they were collected at the time, and what was written alongside them allowed me to piece together Paine's path to recognition, aided with information from the minute book of the excise board and other key documents. This revealed the journey that took Paine eventually on to the world stage, where he has remained ever since.

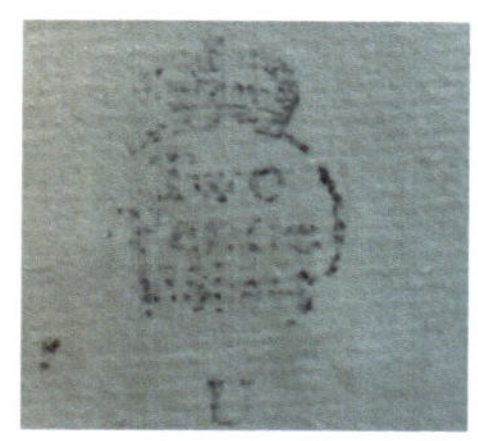 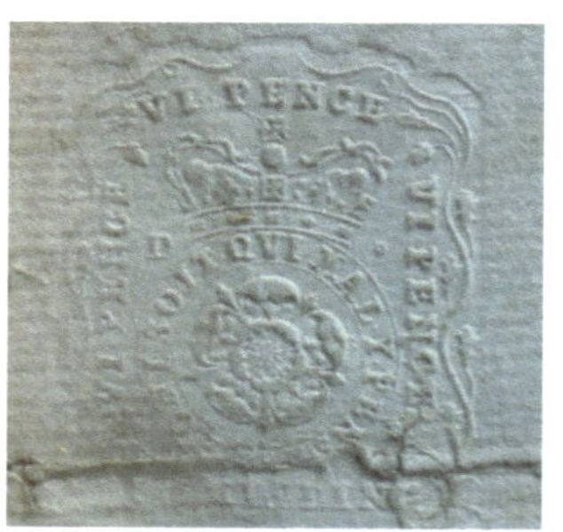

Stamps from the Separation Document